PERFECT T

PERFECT TIMING

The Art of Electional Astrology
by
GREGORY SZÄNTO

THE AQUARIAN PRESS

First published 1989

© GREGORY SZÄNTO 1989

British Library Cataloguing in Publication Data

Szänto, Gregory
Perfect timing: the art of electional
astrology.—(Aquarian astrology handbook
series)
1. Horary astrology
I. Title
133.5'6

ISBN 0-85030-803-8

The Aquarian Press is part of the Thorsons Publishing Group,
Wellingborough, Northamptonshire, NN8 2RQ, England

Typeset by Harper Phototypesetters Limited, Northampton
Printed in Great Britain by Mackays of Chatham, Kent

1 3 5 7 9 10 8 6 4 2

ACKNOWLEDGEMENTS

I acknowledge with grateful thanks the help of the data section of the Astrological Association in providing much of the data which has been the basis of the horoscopes illustrated in this book.

I should also like to thank my wife for her love, help and support and especially in living out the chart elected for our marriage.

GREGORY SZÄNTO

To the Faculty of Astrological Studies, which has done so much to further the cause of serious astrology.

CONTENTS

Let every man be master of his time.
— Shakespeare (*Macbeth*)

PART ONE:
THE THEORY

1.

THE ASTROLOGY OF CHOICE

Taken at the flood: the scope of electional astrology

There is a tide in the affairs of men,
Which, taken at the flood, leads on to fortune;
Omitted, all the voyage of their life
Is bound in shallows and in miseries.

Shakespeare (Julius Caesar)[1]

Electional astrology is the art of choosing the right time for the start of an enterprise. Timing is the essence of life. There is a right time, and a wrong time, for everything. Acting at the right time ensures success. Acting at the wrong time as surely guarantees failure.

The aim of this book is to show how to choose the right time. The potentials of electional astrology, or elections as it is often more succinctly called, are great, greater perhaps than of any other branch of astrology, because it is the only branch of astrology where we have choice, where instead of interpreting an existing horoscope we create one.

However, it is essential that we establish precisely what we are trying to achieve at the outset. Despite the vast potential in this area, despite the unique importance of enabling us to exercise our freedom of choice in actively selecting a time that is right for an enterprise, the ability to elect a horoscope has been largely lost. In the circumstances, it is necessary to start afresh and formulate the rules which are applicable specifically to elections.

What then does choosing the right time for an enterprise mean? It means choosing the time that is right for the *enterprise*. There is a right time, and a wrong time, for every purpose under heaven. This is the central premise of electional astrology, that there is a right time for the enterprise itself. How do we known which is the right time for the enterprise? In order to know the right time, it is necessary first to understand the nature of time. This means understanding how time is composed and how time is reflected in the heavenly bodies which are the tools of astrology.

I have therefore divided this book into two parts. In the first part I shall examine the nature of time and its correlation with the heavenly bodies. Then, in the second part, I shall formulate the rules of choice. For the purposes of elections the nature of time depends on two principles. First, time varies in quality from hour to hour, from day to day, from month to month and over each successive period. Second, every enterprise has its own inherent cycle in time.

Originally elections was one of the four cornerstones of astrology, the other three being mundane, natal and horary. But as regard for the world beyond the confines of the individual became circumscribed, only the latter two branches survived in their original form beyond the seventeenth century. While the reasons can be seen in a general change of perspective over a longer period, the immediate decline in the understanding of elections can be traced back to the time of William Lilly.

It is one of the anachronisms of history that on occasion the preference or antagonism of one person who is regarded as the protagonist of his subject can change the whole pattern for the future. William Lilly's position as the leading astrologer of his age was accepted as unassailable. However, his main interests lay in horary and natal astrology about which he wrote at length, while he was silent on elections. His assistant, Henry Coley, did write extensively about elections, but in doing so he used Lilly's rules on horary and natal astrology which were totally inappropriate for elections.

As a result of this historical accident, horary astrology, which involves setting up a horoscope for the time a question is asked and then trying to read the answer to the question in that horoscope, has gained a popularity which some may feel its potentials hardly warrant. At the same time the principles of elections were confused beyond recognition and thus a branch which had always been recognized as having the greatest practical potentials gradually fell into neglect.

Specifically, the results of using the rules of natal and horary astrology for elections were that, instead of taking the enterprise itself as the starting point and choosing a time which fitted into the natural cycles of that enterprise, the astrologer was encouraged to begin with the horoscope of an individual and then try to accomodate the enterprise to fit that individual's horoscope.

Associating elections with natal astrology entails asking the wrong question. The question then asked is: When is it the right time for John Brown to do something? If this is the question that is really being asked, then the directions of John Brown should be examined to find the best time in his personal cycle. This would then be a case of natal astrology and its rules would apply.

Elections, however, is concerned with the question: When is it the right time for the commencement of this particular enterprise, for founding this university, for launching this rocket, for the inauguration of this peace treaty, so that the enterprise will be a success? This is not to deny that in a particular case it may be necessary to take account of one or more individuals and I shall deal specifically with the issue of comparing the electional horoscope with the horoscope of individuals and indeed of organizations in a later chapter. But the starting point must always be the enterprise for the enterprise itself has its own cycles and its own pattern in time.

Electional astrology is in fact more closely related to the principles of mundane astrology, the other branch which fell into neglect at the same time and which is again becoming increasingly recognized. In mundane astrology the cycles of nations, governments and the affairs of their peoples are studied on the basis that each has its own independent cycle. When the stock market, for example, is examined it can be seen that its cycles operate and correlate with the planetary cycles, independently of those of any individual.

In elections, therefore, we move away from the individual to the state of the world 'out there' or some specific aspect of it. And to understand the nature of this world in time we need to recognize the two underlying aspects of time which I mentioned above: descriptive time and cyclic time as I shall call them in this book.

Descriptive time is based on the premise that each moment has its own quality just as each person and each thing has its own quality. Time and its creations are one. Each child of time, all that is born into a moment of time, has the qualities of that moment of time. This is the basis of astrology in general and it is why we can see the character of a human being by looking at the moment into which he is born. In the same way, when we look at an enterprise its qualities are dependent on the moment of its creation.

Because the universe is a unity the quality of the universe at any time will be reflected in all its parts. An hour that is calm will have its peace infused into every form of existence. It will be mirrored in the gentle stillness of a summer's day, in the steady lapping of waves on the sea shore. And as the planets too are part of the universe, so will the quality of that hour be reflected in their state.

According to the principle of descriptive time, we can choose the quality that is right for an enterprise once we know when and how that quality is reflected by the heavenly bodies. So if in the foundation of a religious establishment we decide that the appropriate qualities are those of permanence, endurance and spiritual stability, we ensure that the planets reflect those qualities. On the other hand, if we are concerned with the merger of a group of textile companies, we would look for qualities to reflect the needs of that particular enterprise.

Cyclic time is based on the premise that events occur and recur according to a definite pattern. Doctors are familiar with the fact that accidents and certain kinds of illness occur in regular cycles. Shakespeare wrote: 'When sorrows come, they come not single spies, but in battalions.'[2] What doctors and dramatists do not know, however, is *when* these events will occur. Without some means of reflection like the planetary bodies whose paths can be accurately forecast, it is not possible to measure the length of the hour or know its coming.

Fay Weldon wrote in her novel *Praxis*: 'Human lives travel through time like the waves of the sea, rising to peaks of experience, falling again, gathering new strength, to rise once more.'[3] Most people are aware of the events in their lives as separate happenings which fall like rain from the sky. Few recognize the pattern of which these seeming events are a part. Fewer realize that the events are woven into the fabric of life itself. There is a pattern beneath the surface of events and it is this pattern which constitutes the deeper reality of our lives infolded in time.

Human existence, with its ebb and flow, its rise and fall, obeys the inherent cycles of its being. All other aspects of life, every principle and every enterprise, have their inherent cycles too. Within these cycles there is a right time and a wrong time, a time that will be easy and a time fraught with difficulty, times of promise and times of delay. Awareness of the cyclic nature of time provides the second means of choice.

The auspicious star: the anatomy of time

'The woman holding a stylus and tablet of the constellations, rapt as it were in thought, was the goddess my sister, Nisaba, showing to you the auspicious star for the building of the temple.'
James Campbell[4]

How is time reflected in the heavenly bodies? Originally it was the descriptive element of time that was most apparent. Our ancestors, being more in touch with the world around them, and their own part in that world, recognized that the state of the universe at any time would be mirrored in whatever happened at that time.

The above quotation is taken from an account of the building of the ziggurat by King Gudea in Sumerian times. It is one of the earliest examples of what was to develop into electional astrology. What is significant about this passage is that the Sumerians, instead of casting a horoscope for the founding of their temple, chose one star and in its symbolism they discovered the time that was right.

If we accept the premise that the universe is a whole, and that therefore the quality of each moment will be reflected in every aspect of the universe, it is logical to choose a single fixed star to describe the quality of an enterprise. In Isaiah we read: 'I have called thee by thy name; thou art mine.' In Sumerian times each child born into the world was the offspring of a star. This was either the fixed star or the planet which rose at the time of his birth.

Each is born under his own star. Similarly when they chose a time for the birth of an enterprise, like the founding of their most sacred temple, it was arranged for it to be born under its own special star. Being born under that star, it would be endowed with its qualities, the qualities which were reflected in the symbolism of the star rising over the horizon. The star under which all creatures were born, whether they were human or inanimate, was symbolically the name of that creature. Just as God calls each creature by his name so that name is reflected in the quality of the universe at the moment that being is born into the world.

The Red Indians too embodied this principle when they named their children according to the quality of the day. They recognized in their wisdom that he who is born in a moment has the qualities and is the living symbol of that moment. They named their offspring 'gentle rain' and 'falling snow', 'bright Sun' or 'boisterous wind' and the child born of that hour would carry the nature of his hour through the timeless span of his life.

Each moment as it falls gives birth to a quality of its own. The Red Indians named the moment and, in naming it, they blessed the child with the quality that fell from the womb in time. Electional astrology does not consist of naming the moment but of creating the moment, of providing the life itself. But to create this life we need to recognize the descriptive reflection of all that exists in time.

The descriptive aspect of time itself consists of two elements. First, the quality of the moment itself. Second, the quality of whatever is born in that moment. In natal astrology the fact that there are two separate elements of descriptive time is glossed over because it is not relevant. There we are only concerned with the person born at a certain time rather than with the time itself and so the latter is subsumed for practical purposes in the former.

Thus we tend to forget that a life born at a certain time is described by the quality of that time, and, unlike the Red Indians, we lose touch with the reality of time. But in elections the time we choose is often important for its own sake, although the degree of importance will depend on the particular enterprise.

Sometimes, with a marriage ceremony for example, it will merely be pleasant to have an agreeable day. In some cases, if a rocket or a ship is being launched, the difference between a good day and a bad day will determine the ability even to begin the enterprise. On other occasions, in a political election, its importance will usually be minimal. But in all cases we shall see the future of the enterprise reflected in the character of the day itself. A day when the elements would seemingly thwart the enterprise, trying almost to hold back its start, bodes ill for the future, whereas the prospects of its future can at other times be foretold by the promise of its inception.

Astrology began to develop into its modern form when the ancients realized two things: first, that the fixed stars were just that, they did not move; second, that the names were not isolated entities but aspects of a recurring pattern. They saw that the qualities they had recognized would return and that they could tell the day of their coming because they formed part of a continuing cycle. When the moving pattern of the planets as well as the Sun and Moon were integrated into these cycles, the beginning of astrology as we known it was born.

The three aspects of time that are relevant in elections and the correlations that exist between the heavenly bodies and time evolved gradually. Taking into account the moving paths of the planets led to the realization that different principles in life, which in turn governed different kinds of enterprise, had cycles of their own and therefore looking at one star alone was no longer viable.

The face of the sky inevitably became more complicated as the factors that were used increased and the relationships between these factors multiplied. It was no longer possible simply to call an enterprise by the name that was symbolized in the quality of a single star. But, as we shall see as we look at the factors in more detail later in this book, the corollary is that we are now able to achieve a far greater range of choice taking account of possibilities contained in the richness of time that were undreamed of by our ancestors.

Walk among the stars: the need for election astrology

> In a higher world it is otherwise but here below to live is to
> change and to be perfect is to have changed often.
>
> J.H. Newman[5]

Why do we need electional astrology? From the brief introduction
above it should be clear that on a mundane level, in the affairs of
daily life, the ability to choose the right time for an enterprise is
vital. In the simplest terms we ensure that we act at the right time
and so succeed in our endeavours.

But the benefit of elections does not stop there, at the mundane
level. Time is an essential element of life. It is not something we
can choose to do without. Whether we like it or not we can only
live in time. The only real choice lies between living consciously as
a part of the underlying pattern of time, accepting the changes that
are inherent in it, its heights and its depths, or being at the mercy
of the events thrown out in its wake.

The more we are in touch with time at the mundane level, the
more we are aware of the different qualities of time. And the more
we learn to do things at the right time, the more we get in touch
with ourselves and with the universe as a whole. For in the process
of everyday living, it becomes clear that time is a real dimension of
life and hence we can see, as did Virginia Woolf, that: 'Life is not
a series of gig-lamps symmetrically arranged; life is a luminous halo,
a semi-transparent envelope surrounding us from the beginning of
consciousness to the end.'[6]

Understanding, and living consciously in the dimension of time,
enables us to alter our perspective of life by recognizing the pattern
that exists within the cycles of time which are reflected in the heavenly
bodies. In this way the changes that can occur only in time can be
realized. As Cardinal Newman said, we can, by changing often, strive
towards perfection.

I began this chapter with a quotation from Shakespeare's *Julius
Caesar*. Caesar himself was perhaps the greatest example of someone
who mastered the art of timing both as a military commander and
as a politician and who, as a result, succeeded brilliantly in his
campaigns and in his political ambitions. According to one of his
biographers[7] his greatest qualities were speed, timing and
flexibility in the face of suddenly changing circumstances. Often
he would snatch victory from defeat by his intuitive grasp of
timing, and so achieved the remarkable success which culminated
in his bestriding 'the narrow world like a Colossus'.

The instinctive awareness that Caesar had of time is something that anyone can learn by understanding the nature and quality of time. But understanding time does mean adopting a new perspective. It is natural to regard time as part of the world 'out there', just as events are seen as aspects of the objective world, things that happen to us, beyond our control, bringing triumph or disaster, and just as the planets circle our world in the sky 'out there'.

In one sense time is an aspect of the objective world. But the more we examine it, and our own life within its span, the more the dividing line between time and human existence breaks down. In ancient mythology three sisters wove the web of life that was the pattern of each creature born into the world from birth to death. In Greek myth the Fates were Clotho who spun, Lachesis who measured the thread, and Attropos whose task was to end man's span by cutting the thread. The Icelanders named their spinners Urdr, Verdandi and Skuld, who collectively represented Past, Present and Future.

Everything that is born into the world, whether human or inanimate, has its pattern, a pattern that exists in time, that has been woven by the three sisters. If we examine the cycles of different phenomena, whether they be the life of an individual or of the stock market, we can see precisely when certain qualities, opportunities, crises, low points and high points, have occurred and will occur. Seeing this pattern enables us to see life in the perspective of time instead of living constantly at the mercy of time and the events that are a part of its stream.

In so far as the pattern exists, we are fated to remain a part of it just as we are fated to remain attached to our physical bodies while we exist on the material level. There is a natural tendency to react negatively to the idea of fate. But in as much as any limitation implies some degree of fate than to that extent fate exists. We cannot fly or live a thousand years and even God cannot change the past. Rather than remonstrate about the limitations that are inevitably a part of life, we can exercise the freedom we have by knowing the measure of the pattern of time as it exists in reality. In doing so we can learn to walk in the shadows as well as through the light.

Understanding the pattern of time as it is enables us to foresee the times that are appropriate for a particular venture and the times that are not. The different qualities contained in these patterns are woven into the web of life and are reflected by the heavenly bodies. We do not create time from nothing. We cannot produce a horoscope that places the heavenly bodies in any position or in any relationship we might wish. We can only arrange the planetary positions as they move through their cycles in the order of time.

The failure to appreciate this has led to the confusion in current electional practice. The purpose of elections is to choose the time inherently right for a particular enterprise according to the natural pattern of that enterprise in time, not to manipulate time by trying to force an artificial composition onto an unwilling enterprise.

All things change in time. Not only do we change but the world itself changes. It changes from day to day and from generation to generation. Change as one season turns into another is clear enough. The fruit dies and falls and replenishes next year's growth. The same pattern takes place among nations, in art and music, in religions, in politics and in commerce. Looking back at the changing world, at fortune and misfortune, at the generations who fought, died and survived wars and pestilence, at the vicissitudes of taste and fashion in literature and painting, we can see these changes emerging.

Sometimes the changes appear to be sudden, to take place in the twinkling of an eye. 'On or about December 1910 human nature changed.' That statement by Virginia Woolf was intentionally enigmatic for we do not expect the subjective world to change in a moment. To say that the world changed on 28 July 1914 would be more understandable because on that day Austria declared war on Serbia.

Yet both changes were always inherent in the pattern of time. That pattern, reflected in the heavenly bodies, could be seen in its totality, not only at the precise moment it erupted in crisis in the form of events but in the seeds sowed as it weaved its circuit around existence, bringing objective and subjective reality together. In December 1910 the two outer planets, Neptune and Uranus, opposed each other from Cancer to Capricorn. The astrologer could see in those positions the dissolution of homes and the destruction of governments.

The seeds sown in that time would grow through one World War until, 29 years later, the span of one Saturn Return, they would give birth to another event that changed the world, the Second World War. Virginia Woolf, looking back with the hindsight of knowledge, could pinpoint that change. Astrologers, with the future knowledge of the planetary positions, can pinpoint the changes that are inherent in the cycles of existence for generations to come. Astrologers too discerned in the first conjunction of Jupiter and Saturn in Pisces two thousand years ago the coming of one who was to embody his generation and fulfil the hopes of his people.

In one sense, by being aware of these changes which are reflected in the planets we get more in touch with time in its objective nature.

In that sense we can regard elections as the complement of therapy. Humanist-existential therapy enables us to make free choices in the world by understanding the interior world of the psyche. Electional astrology, by recognizing time as an aspect of our environment, enables us to make choices in the world outside, in the events and actions of our lives, by understanding the exterior world.

But the more we incorporate time in our lives and learn to do things at the right time, the more we get in touch with the inherent pattern that exists in, and is, our lives. In this way the separation between the objective world 'out there' where events happen to us, and the subjective world 'in here' where we live, begins to dissolve. It is at this point that we should be able to see where electional astrology really leads. From the purely mundane level we are inevitably led, by the very act of getting more closely in touch with the dimension of time, to a greater sense of wholeness, for time is as much a part of the whole as any other dimension of existence.

Timing then consists of using the changes incorporated in the cycles of the planets. The failure to realize this can give the impression that electional astrology involves the manipulation of time. But this idea is based on a fundamental misconception. If time is regarded as something separate from life then we will naturally try to do something to it. We will try to use it because we perceive it as something 'out there'.

Once we recognize time as part of our own lives there is no question of manipulating it or doing anything to an outside dimension. In realizing that we live in time, and that time is the pattern that runs through our lives, we appreciate that we can only choose the right part of our own cycles. Choosing the right time, therefore, means precisely that. It means choosing the time that is right for us and in so far as we choose the right time for an enterprise it means choosing the time that is right for that enterprise.

In this way we align ourselves with the element of time that is central to our lives. In this way we get closer to our real natures and in this way we accept and use the changes that are part of the pattern of our lives. Thus the scope of elections is expanded. What begins as an attempt to ensure success on a mundane level inevitably, as we grow nearer to time as a whole, brings us closer to a vital aspect of our existence. For in doing things at the right time we grow closer to the patterns in time that are woven into the fabric of life. Ultimately, by learning to fulfil the natural pattern of the enterprise and of our lives through the art of timing, we find the reality that lies within the timeless level of the spirit.

2.

THE HISTORICAL DEVELOPMENT

I have described elections as the astrology of choice because elections involves choosing a time for the commencement of an enterprise. In order to exercise such a choice two prerequisites are necessary: first, a belief in the freedom to choose, and second, an understanding of man's relationship with time. As we look at the background of electional astrology we shall see how these two factors affected its development.

Originally, in the cradle of civilization, man was wholly in touch with nature and with time as an integral aspect of that nature. The seasons and the cyclic variations of the year were as natural as they were necessary to his way of life, for his dependence on the weather and other natural phenomena was total. In these circumstances the requirements of agriculture dictated the need to watch the stars, and the planets' rhythmic paths in the sky became symbols of the power of the seasons.

There was no freedom in such a relationship. The most men could do was to watch and try to understand, to predict the future from the pattern of the past and to propitiate the wrath of the gods who controlled their destiny. This fatalistic approach by primitive peoples can be exemplified by the inhabitants of Mexico. Everything done by the Toltecs was subject to the rule of fate and these rules could be found in their magic book, the Teocamoztli, which provided the routine for the conduct of life according to the times and seasons of their calendar.

The Aztecs, whose civilization followed that of the Toltecs, worked out their calendar with meticulous care. They established two series of days ruled by their own gods, the Lords of Time. So each period began with a festival to one of these gods, while the two series coincided every 52 years when the entire cycle began once more. On 2 February, at the beginning of the rainy season, the great festival for the Tlalocs and their sister, Chalchihuitlcue, the water goddess, inaugurated the year.

The relationship of the Norse people to time was no less fatalistic, and indeed their mortal existence can be regarded as a race against time where action and valour alone would endure beyond the inevitable grave. According to their beliefs, creation began when the gods generated time in the form of Night and Day who rode round the heavens in chariots drawn by swift horses. Two fair children, a girl called Sun and a boy called Moon, were also set on paths across the sky, pursued by a pack of ferocious wolves. On the day when the greatest of the wolves succeeded in swallowing the Sun, all things would end.

The Greeks were ambivalent in their attitude towards time and fate. Traditionally, the three sisters, collectively known as Moira, or destiny, controlled even the gods who were themselves aspects of the universe, children of Chaos and Earth as were men. In these circumstances there was no absolute freedom as every form of existence came under the general direction of destiny, but there was a limited freedom within which both gods and men could work their individual wills.

The interrelationship between man's proximity with natural forces and time and his freedom of choice is one which has been a constant thread in the development of electional astrology. Primitive races like the Aztecs were so close to nature that, however much they appreciated the times and the seasons, they were never able to make free choices. Their fatalistic attitude, and incidentally their view of astrology, can be seen from this passage in their book Sahagun, describing the 'day' of Quetzalcoatl, the 13-day period of One Wind: 'If anyone was born on that day they predicted that he would become inhuman, an astrologer and a man with knowledge of how to cast evil spells.'[1]

Gradually, without sacrificing his alignment with nature and time, man lost his primitive fear and evolved a belief in his freedom to direct his life and its enterprises. At this stage astrology, magic and religion were one and the rites which magician and priest celebrated were performed at the times chosen by the astrologer. For the astrologer to achieve this position it was also necessary for him to develop the technical ability to predict the quality and cycles of the heavenly bodies and the evolution of that understanding became another thread that we shall meet as we examine the development of elections.

Belief and superstition: Babylon and Egypt

Although the origins of astrology are uncertain because they precede written records, such evidence as is available leads to Babylon and Egypt, where it appears that the art was developed either independently or with the former culture influencing the latter.

Before the right time could be chosen it was of course necessary to be able to recognize the time that would be beneficial either in general or for a particular enterprise. The early development of astrology therefore reflected a gradual appreciation of the different qualities of time. And this appreciation was obtained from the state of the natural world as a whole before the ancients understood the specific correlation of the planets and other heavenly bodies with circumstances on earth.

Before the Zodiac was invented, as Jack Lindsay points out, the Babylonians looked at nature as a whole and especially at the skies to find an answer to their questions.[2] For them everything in the universe revealed the pattern of time: the weather, the aspects of the sky, dreams, scorpions in the house, the smoke and fire that came from burnt offerings, things that happened to the king as he drove in his chariot.

At this stage then the Babylonians were using what they perceived in the world around them as an omen technique. The basis of their art was the underlying belief that the universe was a unity. Thus everything in the world 'out there', both its general quality and its individual phenomena, reflected what was taking place in the universe as a whole. So, in order to discover what A was doing, or what was going on inside a person's mind, or what was going to happen to B, they looked at the situation in C.

The same development can be seen in other cultures. Among the Aztecs, for example, it was the emperor's function to obtain information from the heavens, for among that people, as among the Chinese, the emperor was regarded as the practical mediator between the divine powers and man because he was so closely in contact with the gods. Thus he observed the sky at sunrise, sunset and midnight. And from the positions of the planets, from the quality and colour of the stars, from any shooting meteorites, displays of the zodiacal light, or mysterious tinted clouds after sunset or before sunrise, he was expected to adduce the quality of the time and the nature of the events which were about to befall. He too would know the flights of birds and the whispering of the wind in the trees.

So the first step in the development of electional astrology was taken. The recognition of the differing quality of the times enabled astrologers, given the technical knowledge to predict when those times would occur and the belief in freedom that enabled them to choose those times, to know which times were right for their enterprises. They appreciated that both the quality of the day as a whole, and also the occurrences during that day, however insignificant they might appear, would reflect the quality of anything that took place on that day.

Initially, therefore, the Babylonians looked at the sky and at nature as a whole in order to be in touch with the quality of the day. As they began to perfect their techniques, their rules became more formal and defined in respect of specific occurrences as well as specific aspects of the sky. On one occasion we find: 'When a yellow dog enters a palace, there will be destruction in its gate. When a piebald dog enters, that place (the king) will make peace with its enemies.'[3]

As the rules became more exact, it was also realized that the particular locality had to be taken into account. Thus, while the sky as a whole reflected the quality of the time, the situation regarding a specific locality depended on what was visible in the sky at that locality. So we read: 'The eclipse of the Moon moved from the eastern quadrant and settled over the whole western quadrant of the Moon. The planets Jupiter and Venus were visible during the eclipse until it cleared. This is propitious for your Majesty and evil for the Westland.'[4]

Although there is no evidence that these rules were used in electional astrology at the time this was written, its relevance should be apparent. For while the quality of the day reflects the quality of any enterprise begun or done on that day as a whole, where there is an adversarial situation, with two or more parties each having opposing needs, it is clear that a time may be good for one party and bad for another. This indeed is what frequently occurred when ambiguous answers were given by oracles without differentiating between the parties.

Two contrasting strands also began to appear at this stage. On the one hand, as more knowledge of the heavenly bodies was acquired, the rules became more refined, while on the other the tendency simply to regard certain days as good or bad quickly degenerated into arbitrary superstition. The result was to provide two different kinds of answer to what was originally the same question. First, we find more exact, and complicated, rules defining the quality of a particular time, while, at the other extreme, we discover a system of auspicious and inauspicious days.

King Eserhaddon, who ruled from 681 to 668 BC, asked his

astrologer whether it would be propitious for the crown-prince to come before him, and if so, whether it would be safe for him to be admitted with a retinue. The answer was: 'They should appear together only in audience. It is excellent: this is the month of Abu and it has many favourable days . . . It is an extremely propitious time for appearing in audience before your Majesty.'[5]

Here we can see both the evolvement of more exact rules and also the belief in good and bad days. The case of King Eserhaddon also reflects the uneasy development of a belief in the freedom of choice which eventually enabled elections to develop, against the older fatalistic assumptions of the primitive mind. In the passage quoted above, the question being asked was not: 'What day will be good for this enterprise?' in the sense of choosing the right day, but rather: 'Will things turn out well or badly on this day for an enterprise that will take place on that day?' Yet we also find the same monarch instructing his astrologers to calculate the best time for the restoration of the images of the gods and rebuilding their sanctuaries.

This dichotomy is also apparent in the case of Seleucus I, King of Babylon in the early third century BC, who was famous for founding cities and whose horoscope for the foundation of the city of Antioch on 22 May 300 BC is one of the earliest examples of an electional Chart in existence. When he consulted astrologers for the time to begin the building of the city named after him, Seleucia, he was told: 'That which is fated, King, neither man nor city can change; for there is a fate for cities as for men.'

At the opposite extreme, a system of good and bad days evolved. In the end this degenerated into the kind of meaningless superstition that makes Friday the 13th unlucky. But initially, before its basis was forgotten, the system was founded on perfectly valid principles. We shall see later that the days of the year are aspects of the solar cycle which vary in quality throughout the year and it was the recognition of this truth that laid the foundation for the arrangement.

In Egypt a system of lucky and unlucky days was produced which then became known as 'Egyptian days' and we find these in use at least into medieval times and even beyond. In Egypt itself the priests marked the days in the calendar for the festivals. Originally the situation was more complicated than it later became for the days themselves were divided into three parts and each part was lucky or unlucky. Thus some days were wholly lucky, others were wholly unlucky, while some were partly lucky and partly unlucky.

Some days too were lucky or unlucky for everything, while others for specific endeavours. For example, it was written of the 5th Phaophi:

'Do not go forth from your house from any side of it and hold no intercourse with women . . . Whoever is born on this day will die of excessive love-making.' And of the 9th it was written that whoever is born on that day will die of old age. On other days, fires should not be lighted nor should songs be listened to.

In Babylon too there were good and bad days but the reasons for these were different from those in Egypt. Initially the Babylonian system was based on the phases of the Moon although in time the original principles were forgotten and arbitrary rules developed. So the four quarter-days were ill-omened and it was unlucky to do business on those days. We shall see later that the intuitive appreciation of this rule was in fact based on solid ground, for the quarter-days mark the phases of the Moon, when this body is in 'hard' aspect to the Sun.

However, it did not take long for these principles to degenerate into arbitrary codes. The Jewish Sabbath was taken over from Babylon with the result that the four quarter-days of the Moon were ill-omened. In Assyria it was forbidden to do any work on the 7th, 14th, 19th, 21st and 28th days of the month. In Babylon itself the week and the month began with the appearance of the sickle Moon in the evening. The time of the beginning and end of this lunar month was especially ill-omened.

Thus the 26th and 27th were days of sorrow and penance, in preparation for the 28th when the Moon crossed the river of death and joined Nergal, the lord of the dead in the darkness of Aralla, while the climax was reached on the 29th which was unlucky for everything. So we read: 'The King shall not go out of the gate . . . If a man goes out on the 29th Nissan he will die, but if he goes out on the 29th Tammuz his wife will die.'

The nature of the gods: Greece and Rome
The affinity with nature that is one of the prerequisites for the development of elections was conceived by the Greeks in a peculiarly rational way. Zenon described the goal of human existence as 'life in accordance with nature'.

This philosophy may be summed up in the words of Diogenes Laertios:

Living virtuously is equivalent to living in accordance with experience of the actual processes of nature . . . For our individual natures are part of the nature of the whole universe. And that is why the end may be defined as life in accordance with nature, or, in other words, in accordance with our own human nature as well as with that of the universe, a life in which we refrain from every action forbidden by the law common to all things, i.e. the right reason which pervades all things and is identical with this Zeus, Lord and Ruler of all that is. And this very thing constitutes the virtue of the happy man and the smooth current of life, when all actions promote the harmony of the spirit dwelling in the individual man with the will of him who orders the universe.[6]

The concept of man's essential unity with the universe as a whole and the rightness of his actions in accordance with the greater pattern of nature could not be better put. However, the very act of producing these ideas had the paradoxical effect of separating the Greeks from nature by creating, through their minds, an artifical gulf which divided them from the objective world they had inadvertently created.

While their affinity with nature developed, albeit conceptually, the seeds of superstition were also increasing. It was in the Hellenistic era that the days of the week were given their planetary attributes. Saturday, as the day of Saturn or Satan, was felt to be especially malevolent. Then the question of free will found the Greeks divided into two schools. One held that everything was predetermined, while the other, the 'catharchic', that only certain things were predetermined and by studying the movement of the planets propitious times could be chosen.

As early as the eighth century BC, Hesiod wrote in his *Works and Days* that the planets and stars should be used to predict good times at which to start certain tasks. And by the end of the Hellenistic era, the casting of city horoscopes for laying the foundation stones of cities had become common. Constantinople, Alexandria, Gaza, Caesaria and Neopolis, for example, were all founded on the principles of electional astrology.

Other examples of elections in the mundane sphere at this time were the coronations of rulers. Antiochus I Epiphanes of Kommagare had his coronation fixed for the 6 or 7 July 62 BC on the advice of his astrologers. The limits of free will can also be seen in the stories, albeit apocryphal, of astrologers trying to choose the right time for the birth of their future rulers. That of Nektanebos is perhaps the best known. He is said to have begged the mother of Alexander the Great to hold back from giving birth until an auspicious time had arrived, and then, when the child was about to be born, saying, no doubt with relief, 'Queen, you will now give birth to a ruler of the world.'

The Romans who, lacking the extreme rational qualities of the Greeks, were more concerned with practical matters, enhanced the constructive development of their predecessors' ideas. Among this race too we find on the one hand a heightened acceptance of the idea of unity with the universe, while on the other, a resort to blatant superstition.

Roman religion was based on the premise of mutual trustfulness, or *fides*, between the divine powers or gods above and human beings on earth. From earliest times in Rome all things were felt to be subordinate to divine rule and direction and it was accepted that this trust was accorded by the gods through their benevolence. There was a sense of absolute order which worked out the divine law of the universe and thus their religion, and beliefs as a whole, were based on the principle of propitiation which made the step from faith to fate a short and inevitable one.

There was a unity here between heaven and earth, but no longer the intimate indivisibility of the Babylonians – rather the rational reflection that owed its influence to the Greeks which demanded conscious reciprocity. The Romans sought the peace of the gods, or *pax deorum*, which was the balance of nature in which the divine powers and human beings worked in detail and in order to obtain this they evolved and observed meticulous ritual.

What choice was there in these circumstances? The dilemma between fate and free will, between being so close to the universe in its oneness that the individual had no choice, and in being the master of his own destiny, led to an uneasy compromise. As Tacitus put it: 'So law does not depend on the course of the wandering planets but is fixed in the first principles of things, supported and sustained by a chain of natural causes. Man all the same is left at liberty to choose his sphere of action; but, once the choice is made, the consequences follow in a regular course, fixed, certain, inevitable.'[7]

In practice the Roman attitude was extremely fatalistic, and this was true not only among the market-place astrologers but also among the more learned practitioners. A system of lucky and unlucky days, reminiscent of the Egyptian system, was evolved. *Dies fasti* were those open for public business. *Dies comitiales* were available for election-assemblies unless they coincided with one of the *mundinae* or holidays. When there were no public meetings legal transactions took place on these days, while on *dies nefasti* no public business of any kind was allowed.

Auspicious times were also chosen in accordance with the gradually evolving principles of elections and we find Balbillus choosing an auspicious moment for Nero to be proclaimed Emperor. It was in medicine in particular that the more serious principles of elections were used as they were to continue to be used for centuries to come. Galen himself, perhaps the greatest of medical practitioners, insisted that the theriac, a medicine he had developed, should be taken at the third hour of the 1st or 4th day of the Moon.

Magic and the medieval world

It was in medieval times that astrology, and in particular elections, met its foremost critic in the form of the Christian Church. Yet the Church's attitude towards astrology was for the most part ambivalent, and its attempt to reconcile its beliefs with the basis of astrology was never successful.

The main divergence between Christian doctrine and what the Church regarded as pagan belief was that in the old religions the spirit of God was immanent in nature as a whole and the various attributes of this spirit were personified in the form of the gods. So nature, and the universe, was a whole where all things reflected each other. Judaism, and hence Christianity, on the other hand, worshipped a God outside and above nature, a creator who stood apart from his creatures.

The view of God as separate from nature affected both the prerequisites for electional astrology that I mentioned in Chapter 1. But while the relationship between God, man and nature caused many of the unresolved difficulties in Christian acceptance of astrology, it was on the issue of free will that most of the ostensible problems revolved.

Initially, however, these divergences were not apparent, mainly because Christianity was simply imposed on the old religions with little change of underlying belief, the pagan gods and festivals being taken over and renamed to accomodate their successors. Thus it was recognized that certain times were auspicious because the quality of the times changed and these changes were reflected in the heavenly bodies.

It was also in the field of medicine that we continue to find examples of such astrological knowledge. In this country, for example, there is this account by a late seventh-century bishop: 'You did very indiscreetly and unskilfully to bleed her in the fourth day of the Moon; for I remember that Archbishop Theodore, of blessed memory, said that bleeding at that time was very dangerous, when the light of the Moon and the tide of the ocean is increasing; and what can I do to the girl if she is like to die?'[8]

Later the Church, in trying to implement its views on free will, distinguished between certain kinds of astrology. The distinction was made between 'natural astrology', the study of celestial phenomena and terrestial events, and 'judicial astrology', which included nativities, horaries and elections, as the latter relied on the creation of horoscopes for interpretation. The basis of this rationale was that in the former, the astrologer merely interpreted something which already existed, while in the latter, he first created a horoscope in order to interpret it.

However, a little thought will show that the apparent difference between these two categories is no more than a matter of degree. When the astrologer sets up a natal chart he is merely inserting the positions of the heavenly phenomena as they exist in the sky. He is no more creating something than the person who takes a photograph of an existing scene. The same is true of horaries, where the astrologer interprets the heavenly phenomena at the moment a question is asked.

The only kind of astrology where a horoscope is created in a real sense is elections, for here alone the astrologer exercises choice in producing the most propitious chart he can devise. Here therefore one can more readily understand the Church's opposition to astrology, even if one does not agree with the basis of its contentions. Another reason for the Church being opposed to elections in particular was its intimate connection with magic. The dilemma facing the Church in this context was that during the medieval period people instinctively accepted the unity of nature as the basis of God's presence in the world and in their lives and thus the validity of magic and astrology continued to be central to their belief system.

It is indeed important to appreciate the basis of this belief system in order to see how elections evolved and also the reason for the Church's attitude. Astrology and magic were then two parts of one system and electional astrology in particular was the time element of magic. The underlying tenet of this belief system was that there are certain natural laws which all aspects of nature, including man, obey because all are parts of the whole. Therefore whatever happens in one part of the system is reflected in all other parts.

Astrology, apart from elections, was concerned with interpreting these natural laws. So in natal astrology the astrologer would see the character of the human being born at a certain time reflected in the pattern of the heavenly bodies which existed at that time. Magic went further than this, for the purpose of magic was to bring about changes in accordance with the will. In theory this is where the Church should have opposed magic for such changes could upset the laws of nature. But Jesus himself constantly made references to such changes, even stating that if a person had sufficient faith he could move mountains.

In fact, although the magician believes in the possibility of making any change provided his will is sufficiently strong, what he tries to do in practice is to bring about these changes at the times which are right for the particular purpose, for he recognizes that it is much easier to work with a force, or natural law, than against it, as anyone who enjoys sailing will appreciate. In these circumstances it was the task of the electional astrologer to discover the times which were right, or in accordance with such natural laws, for a particular enterprise. So while in practice it was Jesus and his disciples who healed the sick at all times, the principles of elections were used by Christian and pagan alike in medieval times to heal at the most natural times.

While for the most part magic and astrology were used in conjunction, on occasion the two drew apart when, rather than using astrology to choose the right time, the magician attempted to manipulate time. We can see examples of both uses in one of the foremost astrologer-magicians of the medieval age, Guido Bonati, who lived in thirteenth-century Italy.

Bonati used elections proper to choose the best times for the various enterprises of his patron, Guido da Montefeltro. These included public affairs, laying foundation stones and, in particular, starting the military campaigns of da Montefeltro. In pursuit of the latter he would, having chosen the right time, mount the tower of the church of San Mercuriale, and ring the bell for his patron's advance against the enemy.

There are a number of amusing stories about Bonati which illustrate both sides of his activities. As an example of his electional art, he was asked to help with the construction of new walls at Forli and he decided that he would use this operation as an opportunity to bring about the reconciliation of the two warring parties, the Ghibellines and the Guelfs. In the event a member of each party was chosen for the ceremony and both were instructed to hold a foundation stone while the masons stood by with mortar, until Bonati gave the order for their laying at the decisive moment. When the signal was duly given, the Ghibelline laid his stone but the Guelf, suspecting a trick, withheld his. Thereupon Bonati cursed the Guelfs, saying that the right moment would not be repeated for another 500 years. No doubt he looked back with satisfaction when the Guelfs were later destroyed.

The manipulation of time can be seen in the magical use of images. When an image is made at a certain time, astrologically chosen, it is like a natal chart in that it contains the potential of that time. The theory was that the image would then keep the influence and could be used at a later time, and the theory was extended when parts of the image were made at one appropriate time, while others were made at another.

The artificial production of images can be traced back at least to the tenth century. Thabit ibn Kurrah, astrologer to the Caliph of Baghdad, a contemporary of King Alfred, stated: 'When you want to make an image for a man who wishes to become the head of a city or province, or judge of a prefecture or a town, the method is the same . . . Carve the head of the image under whatever rising sign the Moon shall be in, carve the shoulders and breasts with Venus in the Ascendant, the haunches with the Sun rising in one of its dignities, the thighs with Mercury in the Ascendant, and he must not be retrograde or combust, but should be unafflicted in one of his fortunate places, and the feet under Ascendant of the Moon in conjunction with Venus, etc.'[9]

When Bonati was asked by an apothecary to help him regain his weath, he made a wax image and told the apothecary to hide it carefully and not to speak of it to anyone. The apothecary then regained his wealth but made the mistake of telling a priest who said the image must be destroyed. Having done so, the apothecary lost his wealth once more and so returned to Bonati. On asking Bonati to make him another image, the apothecary was told that the right time would not occur for another 50 years.

We can see here how magic and astrology began to part company, for the time itself and the creatures of that time became separated and, like Frankenstein's monster, the one no longer depended upon the other. In the case of Bonati's image, the time had become attached to the image. According to the principles of elections, if Bonati had merely chosen the right time for the apothecary to begin his search, then the fact that something happened later to the image created at that time would have had no effect. We shall see in the next section how elections and images continued to run in paths parallel to each other.

On the other hand, elections in their 'pure' form were used by the time of Bonati's *Liber Astronomicus* to choose the favourable moment for virtually any and every human activity, including trimming one's nails, and lists were made of good years for monarchs, bishops and growing cucumbers. In the twelfth century, Daniel of

Morley wrote on elections choosing the auspicious moment for a ship sailing on an important voyage.

In medicine too the art was used in every aspect of its practice: the right moment for applying the medicine, for performing the operation and for raising the patient from bed. Andalo di Negro wrote on the best time to administer laxatives and for bleeding and in 1358 Bishop Ugo de Costello wrote a book on 'critical days' of illness. Equally we find the use of sympathetic magic when Peter of Padua advised that the figure of a scorpion should be made when the Moon is in the Sign of the Scorpion to cure the bite of that creature.

The natural sympathy and correspondence that continued to connect magic and astrology during this period was deeply interwoven and could be simple or complicated. A spell against gout ends: 'Do it when the Moon is in the constellation of the Lion.' While at the other extreme, a talisman for lordship and dominion should be made when the Ascendant is in Leo, the Sun in 13 degrees of Aries, the Moon in 3 degrees of Taurus, Saturn in Aquarius, Jupiter in Sagittarius, Mars in Virgo and the metals of the planets concerned should be melted on a Thursday morning in the hour of Jupiter.

The schism: the Renaissance and after

The zenith precedes its decline. High summer, when the Sun stops, presages in its fullness the shortening of the day and the advent of autumn. The Renaissance marked the height of astrological influence and the refinement of previous techniques. To contemporaries, it seemed that their art had reached an apotheosis that would ensure in its continued survival a vigorous proliferation into the future.

But the times, as always, were changing. The curiosity of the age turned away from man's intimate relationship with the universe and looked out into a new objective world which quickly turned into modern scientific materialism. Having achieved the freedom to choose which was so essential to the art of elections, man freed himself from his old perceptions.

The limited horizons of medieval minds were widening, helped by the new knowledge coming from the East, mainly through Arab culture. Although magic and astrology, so intimately connected until now that astrology was regarded by the magician as merely the time element of his art, were both beginning to decline, at the same time astrologers developed a greater interest in natural events. Having recognized the quality of the day from the Moon and diurnal factors in the sky, they learned to read in the great conjunctions of the planets,

and especially those of Saturn, Jupiter and Mars, the signs and courses
of great historical events.

John of Seville translated the work of the great Arabian scholar,
Albumasar, who lived in ninth-century Baghdad and died in 886,
and this translation was published in 1489 in Augsburg and in 1515
in Venice. Another Arab, Ibn Kaldun, synthesized the ideas of
Albumasar, Ptolemy and Al-Battani in a work known as *The
Mugaddimah: An Introduction to History*. In it he wrote: 'For matters
of general importance such as royal authority and dynasties, they
use the conjunctions, especially those of the two superior planets
. . . Saturn and Jupiter . . . The conjunctions of the two superior
planets are divided into great, small and medium. The great
conjunction indicates great events, such as a change in royal authority
or dynasties, or a transfer of royal authority from one people to
another.'[10]

In the fourteenth century, John of Eschenden wrote in his *Summa
iudicalis de accidentibus mundi* that the great conjunctions were
the signs and causes of the plague. Tycho Brahe also wrote to the
same effect: 'In 1593, when a great conjunction of Jupiter and Saturn
took place in the first part of the Lion, near to one of the nebulous
stars in Cancer, which Ptolemy calls the smoky and pestilent ones,
did not the pestilence which swept over the whole of Europe in the
years that followed, and caused innumerable people to perish,
confirm the influence of the stars by a very certain fact?'[11]

Medieval and Renaissance magic were both based on similar
assumptions, that the universe was conceived as ordered, earth-
centred and astrological. According to these ideas the stars were living
creatures influencing the actions of everything on earth and there
was a natural sympathy and antipathy between all things. Natural
magic, as it was called, was based on the belief that the heavenly
bodies were superior organisms through which God channelled his
powers, and the magician operated by manipulating the powers of
the astral bodies through sympathy.

For example, to attract the powers of the Sun, he needed to know
which plants, stones, metals etc. were sympathetic and thus the
complicated system of correspondences which can be found in the
pages of magical grimoires was built up. So Sun talismans were made
at the correct astrological times.

The use of talismans and images had reached the point where
it appeared that they would take over the role of elections and
astrology would be completely subsumed in magic. In the fifteenth
century Marsilio Ficino was capturing the celestial powers in the image

on the analogy of the simulacrum, for by capturing and making use of the celestial powers at the right time their power was preserved like a fly in amber. As De Vita wrote: 'To fight a fever one sculpts Mercury in marble, in the hours of Mercury, when Mercury is rising, in the form of a man who bears arrows.'[12] And we read in *Speculum astronomiae*: 'I have said that the science of images, not of every kind but of astronomical ones, has, however, replaced part of the elections.'[13]

However, the tide turned once more and, while magic and astrology remained in close proximity, they also pursued their separate paths. John Dee was perhaps the last of the great astrologer-magicians who tried, unsuccessfully as it turned out, to bridge the ancient and modern worlds. He wrote: 'We, also, daily may perceive, that mans body, and all other Elementall bodies, are altered, disposed, ordred, pleasured and displeasured by the Influentiall working of the *Sunne*, *Mone*, and other Starres and Planets.'[14] But, although he elected the time for Elizabeth I's coronation on 15 January 1559 and was that Queen's official court astrologer, he died in poverty, an anachronism from another age.

For astrology was breaking away from magic as the sixteenth century turned into the seventeenth. During those centuries there were four main branches of astrology: general predictions, nativities, elections and horary. During this time too the Church's attitude towards astrology in general, and elections in particular, was more favourable. When Pope Paul III was elected he installed Luca Gaurico as unofficial astrologer to the papacy, creating him Bishop of Giffoni, and the new bishop then elected the time for laying the cornerstone of new buildings in the neighbourhood of St Peter's, at which a grand ceremony was held with a cardinal laying the marble slab.

Pope Alexander VI, perhaps better known as Roderigo Borgia, used electional astrology to plan his military campaigns. And his great rival, Pope Julius II, had the time of his coronation selected on the basis of elections. That Pope also ordered an astrologer to elect an auspicious time for laying the foundation stone of the castle of Galliera and for the erection of his statue at Bologna.

In the seventeenth century astrologers were choosing appropriate days for launching ships and for the beginning of their clients' voyages, and indeed by the middle of the eighteenth century it had become customary in North America for a horoscope to be cast to decide on sailing dates. In this country John Flamsteed chose 10 August 1675 to lay the foundation for the Royal Observatory at Greenwich.

The time of Charles II was one when elections were used sometimes in their pure form and sometimes in conjunction with magical principles. Thus Charles himself consulted Elias Ashmole for an astrologically propitious moment for delivering a speech to Parliament on 27 October 1673, and John Ogilby too asked Ashmole for the best time to begin learning Greek. If the Merry Monarch did not entirely believe in astrology's efficacy, and he was certainly unimpressed when he asked an astrologer to tell him which horse would win at his favourite Newmarket races, Ashmole was without doubt a fervent practitioner of both astrology and magic.

He stated: 'Judicial astrology is the key of natural magic, and natural magic the door that leads to this blessed stone.'[15] On this basis he made sigils and talismans at astrologically propitious times, which he stored and used later. As Keith Thomas put it: 'Appropriate heavenly influences were caught like fruit as they fell and stored up for use when needed. By capturing these astral emanations, the astrologers could divert the power of the heavens to their own ends.'[16] So Ashmole used them against fleas and mice which were infesting his house and against his wife's attacks of vomiting. And as Parliamentary candidate for Lichfield in 1678 he cast sigils 'for the increase of honour and estimation of great men'.

As the times progressed the original situation with regard to the two prerequisites of elections was reversed. Whereas there had been an intuitive understanding of man's relationship with nature but no belief in his freedom of choice, now the freedom to choose had been attained but in the process the understanding of the relationship between the heavens above and the earth below had been lost. The result was that the principles upon which elections had been based, the appreciation of the quality of time and its variations which were reflected in the heavenly bodies, were forgotten.

In these circumstances there was a general reversion to the superstitious reliance on lists of dates which were as useless as the so-called 'Egyptian days'. The serious astrologers who continued to practise at this time showed little, if any, interest in elections and consequently, as a result of Lilly's neglect in particular, the rules which were later resurrected were no longer based on valid principles.

The tendency to produce good and bad days, either in general or for particular enterprises, can be seen as a thread running through the centuries. In medieval times the system of 'Egyptian' or 'dismal' days grew up and proliferated but it became uncertain which days were referred to and why, as rival sets of conflicting dates got into circulation.

This credulous approach can be seen in as sensible, not to say

sceptical, a man as Lord Burghley who wrote to his son, in 'Advice
to his Son': 'Though I think no days amiss to undertake any good
enterprise or business in hand, yet have I observed some, and no
mean clerks, very cautious to forbear . . . three Mondays in the
year.'[17] These were the first Monday in August, the anniversary of
the death of Abel, the second Monday in August, being the
destruction of Sodom and Gomorrah, and the last Monday in
December, which was the birthday of Judas Iscariot.

Church festivals were associated with such days and so Friday was
unlucky because it was the day of the crucifixion. On that day, a
person should not marry, make a journey or cut his nails, nor should
he shoe or plough; he could pick stones but not disturb the soil.
St Loy's day too was bad for shoeing horses, and John Aubrey wrote:
'We dread to do business on Childermass Day.'

By the seventeenth century almanacs were being produced which
listed favourable days for blood-letting, purging, bathing, the right
and wrong times for agricultural operations – planting, sowing,
mowing, gelding – as well as generally 'unlucky' days. That this advice
could cause trouble was apparent when in 1666 six ex-Parliamentary
soldiers were involved in a republican plot, having chosen a day for
their enterprise from Lilly's almanac.

The rules which were in use at this time perhaps reached their
most inflexible nature in Joseph Blagrave's *Introduction to Astrology*
in 1682 which included precepts for knowing when to engage in
a lawsuit, fight a duel or propose a marriage, and 'how to choose
a fit time to visit any kinsman, brother or neighbour, so as to obtain
any thing desired from them.'

Thomas, in his masterly account of this period, writes: 'Yet for
all its apparent subjectivity, astrology left everything in the last resort
to the judgement and common sense of the practitioner, and the
system, far from being exact, was highly flexible. As with many kinds
of divination, there were rules to be followed, but their interpretation
was ultimately subjective.'[18]

To an extent this was true. The effective practitioners, such as there
were, relied on their intuition to see the real principles behind the
rules. The rules themselves, however, had to a very large extent become
more exact, rigid and inflexible and it became increasingly difficult
to discover the principles behind them. It is for this reason that if
electional astrology is once again to be restored to its rightful place
as one of the cornerstones of astrology its principles must again be
discovered, and in the process much of the irrelevant dogma needs
to be jettisoned.

3.
THE ANALYSIS OF TIME

This little sphere: science and the frontiers of time

One hour is not identical to another, for conditions in space change. Our determinants are not confined to earth; our life is not bound by the simple measurements which pertain to the surface of this little sphere. It expands to the dimensions of the universe. Man's measure has become the cosmos.

Michel Gauquelin[1]

In 1951 Professor Giorgio Piccardi, director of the Institute of Inorganic Chemistry at the University of Florence, made some remarkable discoveries. Over a period of years he monitored the rate of time that a colloid, oxychloral bismuth, took to dissolve. He found that the reaction speed varied according to the time of day, month and year. In March, for instance, independently of weather or other external conditions, the reaction would suddenly speed up. Conversely in September it would slow down dramatically.

Experiments of equal significance were being carried out on living creatures by J.C. Jahuda. In a series of tests on grasshopper mice, Jahuda confirmed that the activity of the mice varied markedly at different times, and moreover that these times coincided with the phases of the Moon. He found that the mice were most active between the last and first quarters and least active at the Full Moon. Furthermore, he noticed that during the first quarter they had their peak activity in the evening, while during the last quarter their peak took place during the morning.

Professor Piccardi summed up his findings in these words: 'Our research . . . will be able to show how man is linked to his environment with bonds that escape his immediate apprehension, if not his awareness. Only by understanding the mechanism that connects him to the earth and the sky will man be able to understand better his physical and psychic position in the universe today. In the context of the universe as it is, man will find his natural role.'[2]

In the days of Newton it was accepted that time was a continuum, a never changing backdrop of unanimity against which the flow of events occurred. In the light of modern scientific research it has become clear first that the quality of time itself varies, and second that there is a correlation between the quality of time and the heavenly bodies. Events no longer happen in time. Events and time are indissolubly linked.

The fact that time itself varies became apparent to Professor Piccardi as a result of his experiments with 'activated' water. This water was used to descale boilers and, given the uniform conditions that existed throughout the work, the operation should have been carried out at a uniform rate. It was naturally expected, for example, that when the water reached its freezing point it would invariably freeze. But this is not what happened. At certain specific times the water failed to freeze at a temperature several degrees below its freezing point. It became clear that there was a marked variation in the quality of the water depending on the time of the day, month and year.

Once it is realized that there is a connection between the events and the time in which they occur the variation in the quality of time can be examined in greater detail. However, without some kind of measuring device it is virtually impossible to see precisely how time varies, let alone foretell when a particular kind of time will occur.

But with the realization that the quality of time is reflected in the heavenly bodies it is possible to analyse the variations of time in the greatest detail and also to see when these times will occur in the future. In this chapter therefore we shall be concerned with the analysis of time. We shall see how its quality varies and how these variations are reflected in the heavenly bodies.

Once scientists found that time varied in quality, that it changed in nature like any other aspect of existence, they went on to discover that these variations occurred according to specific patterns so that any particular quality would be repeated according to a specific cycle. The cyclic aspect of time became apparent to Professor Piccardi when he carried out his experiments on oxychloral bismuth and activated water. The correlation between the activity of Jahuda's grasshopper mice and the cycles of the Moon became increasingly clear to him as his experiments developed.

The cycles of the Moon and the Sun are apparent to anyone because these bodies can readily be seen in the sky. We can hardly fail to be aware of the annual seasons if not of the Moon's phases. While the cycles of the planets are not immediately accessible unless we specifically look for them, their paths can be traced in the available tables without difficulty.

In the varying quality of time and in the recurring pattern of change we see the two aspects of time which I discussed in Chapter 1. I shall examine these two elements in the following two sections of this chapter. Both aspects can be seen in the correlation between the heavenly bodies and the situation on earth. In the descriptive aspect we can see the quality that is right for a particular kind of enterprise. In the cyclic aspect we can see the right time in the evolution of the enterprise itself.

The emphasis on these two aspects will differ depending on the specific nature of the enterprise, for each is dependent on a different viewpoint of the heavenly bodies as they are symbolized in astrology. Time in its descriptive role originates in a reflective perspecitve of astrology, while time in its cyclic role has its basis in astrology as the time element of magic when it was necessary to choose the right time for performing a particular ceremony.

Our ancestors appreciated that timing was vital in their operations, and that without a knowledge of the different qualities of time the chances of success would be minimal. Today, although the language has changed, the principles remain the same. The realization of the constituents which govern time are as necessary as they have always been. At the mundane level this realization can mean quite simply the difference between life and death. Finally this is being recognized by medical practitioners. Professor Alain Reinberg has recently been experimenting at the National Centre for Scientific Research in France on the effectiveness and toxicity of medicine taken at different times.

When he divided a number of mice into two groups and gave the same toxic substance to each at different times he found a significant divergence in the effects. One group was given the substance at 4 p.m. and 80 per cent died. But when the other group was given the substance at midnight 90 per cent survived. The results of these experiments have laid the foundation for the new science of chronotherapy.

With this knowledge, Dr Henri Levy at the Villejuif Hospital went on to devise a timetable for the treatment of specific cancers, having discovered that white blood cells vary from a proportion of one to six during the day according to a precise cycle. It has also been found that the effects of anaesthetics and steroids vary considerably depending on the time of day according to clear cycles. So important is timing in diagnosis that Professor Reinberg has said: 'If you don't know at what time the sample is taken, it is impossible to interpret the results.'

Yet these discoveries are not new. In 1427 we find St Bernardino of Siena writing: 'You will see that when you want to give medicine to an invalid, the doctor says: "It is good to give it to him on such a day; and by giving it to him on the day it is safe, it will do him good; and by giving it to him on another day, and not being careful about the days on which you do it, you could do him harm." '[3]

The importance of timing in medicine is perhaps most obvious. But on every level of life the rediscovery of timing can lead not only to success and well-being on the material level but to an insight and alignment with an integral element of life. The need has again been stressed by Michel Gauquelin: 'Time, then, is not an identical continuum without meaning for animals and things. It is a coordinate in the proper sense of the word, like length, breadth, temperature and pressure. By forgetting to ask time to participate in their experiments scientists are in the position of the parents of Sleeping Beauty.'[4]

The descriptive approach
In this section and the next I am going to examine the two approaches to time: time as descriptive and time as cyclic. Descriptive time rests on two premises. The universe is a whole and it changes in nature from moment to moment. Because the universe is a whole its quality is described by all phenomena including the heavenly bodies. Because life is motion the universe is in a constant state of change as it moves through time.

How can we see this constantly changing quality of time? How is it described? What are the factors that make up the whole? And how do we use these factors to create the kind of time we want? These are the questions we shall be answering. First, however, let us pause to see how the universe is described at any time and what this means in the context of elections.

One morning we wake up to a languid sense of peace, the world revolves in slow motion, the sun intruding through a soporific haze. The atmosphere is muted, nature slumbers. Voices are hushed, the telephone silent, the baby paddles contentedly and the cat crawls over the bedspread. The next day we spring out of bed, galvanized by a sense of urgency, head thumping with the hammering of a teenager's electric guitar, dustmen banging bins in the street outside. We scrape the car on the garage door and arrive at the office to confront an irate client and a tearful secretary.

It is *that* kind of day. And *that* kind of day will produce events of a similar nature because the quality of time pervades the universe and all that happens in it. When Martin Luther King arrived in Memphis on 3 April 1968 to give what was to be his last address, thunder crashed over the city, there had been a bomb scare on his plane and his mood matched the threatening storm and the lashing rain. Within a few hours he had been assassinated. In the atmosphere of the day we can see both the quality of the events which occur on that day and the character of the enterprise which will develop in time according to the nature of its birth.

We can recognize a particular quality simply by being open to the atmosphere of the day or the hour. We, however, are concerned not only with recognizing the quality of the time, but of knowing the hour of its coming. Because the quality of time is reflected in the heavenly bodies as it is in all other aspects of nature, and because we can see precisely where these bodies will be at any time in the future, they make the perfect correlation for knowing when any particular quality will exist in the future. All we need to know is how the heavenly bodies do correlate with the quality of the times.

So let us see how this correlation works. Then we can choose both the quality of the day itself and so achieve a day that is right and also arrange a particular quality for the start of the enterprise which will be the seed of the enterprise as a whole.

The factors which reflect the quality of time are the Signs of the Zodiac, the Sun, Moon, planets and Angles, the aspects, and the Houses. The underlying quality of the time is reflected in the Signs of the Zodiac. The Sun, Moon, planets and Angles represent the duration of these qualities. The aspects modify the qualities, while the Houses show how they will operate in the mundane sphere.

Let us now take these four features in turn. First, the Signs of the Zodiac. It is here that we can see the general character of time. The 12 Signs contain the whole range of underlying qualities from which to choose a particular kind of time, just as we can choose from a number of primary colours when we paint a picture. When the Signs are activated their qualities will be revealed for a particular period.

I shall look at the individual Signs in detail in Chapter 5 when we shall see examples of the kinds of events they throw up, and in Part Two I shall be looking at specific ways of using these qualities. At this stage we can se how the 12 Signs are made up. The Signs represent ways the energies that exist in life manifest and they are the result of a breakdown of the total energy that is in existence by the first four numbers, the numbers themselves being the governing principles of the universe and of all life.

The Zodiac in its collective state is one. Where there is no division there is no life and only in the Godhead is there unity and eternity. For life to come into existence there must be motion and change. When the whole, the unity of the Zodiac, splits into two we have the polar energies of yang and yin, the active and the receptive. It is upon these two pillars that all life is based.

This primary division produces the Signs alternatively from the first to the last. Thus the first Sign, Aries, is yang, followed by a yin Sign, Taurus. Then Gemini is yang and Cancer yin and so on throughout the whole cycle. So the ebb is followed by the flow, the peak by the trough, the breath out by the breath in. So life obeys the first principle of giving and receiving and the one is always followed by the other as life rises and falls to rise again.

After the two comes the three. When the cycle of the Signs is divided by three we get the four Elements. Each Element therefore comprises three Signs. It was of these four Elements that the ancients believed the world and all life to be composed, and imbalance and disease were, in their view, the result of some lack of harmony between these four energies in man or in some other facet of the world.

Although we no longer believe the world to be literally composed of the four Elements, nevertheless as principles and as aspects of human temperament they do reflect reality. They are important in natal astrology because they reflect the temperament of the individual, and they are also important in elections because they reflect the overall quality of a particular time.

When one of the yang Signs is activated, the time will be outgoing, enterprising. Conversely, when one of the yin Signs is activated, the time will be receptive, incoming. Now because there are four Elements and two polarities, two of the Elements are yang, and two yin. So the Fire Element, which consists of the Signs Aries, Leo and Sagittarius, is yang, as are the Air Signs Gemini, Libra and Aquarius.

Equally the Water Signs, consisting of Cancer, Scorpio and Pisces, are yin, as are the Signs in the Earth Element, which are Taurus, Virgo and Capricorn. The Fire Signs are active in a physical, assertive way. They are filled with creative energy and the natural exuberance of life, radiating a sense of enthusiasm, vigour and magnetism. The Air Signs are active in a more refined, mental way. They reflect times of communication, of relating through words and speech, in a rational, linear manner.

When we come to the yin Elements, the tide turns inwards. The

Water Element draws to itself emotionally, through human feeling; it stirs the imagination and the sense of other worlds, of the spirit, of art and humankind. The Earth Element draws us to the earth itself, to practical affairs, to the daily world of bringing down into manifestation, of work and craftsmanship, of practical endeavour.

Finally we reach the number four. Dividing the circle of 12 by this number produces the three Modes or Quadruplicities. Each of the three Signs in each Element acts according to the nature of one of these Modes: the Cardinal, the Fixed and the Mutable. These too form a continuous cycle. So the first Sign, Aries, is Cardinal of the Element Fire, while the next, Taurus, is Fixed, of the Element Earth, and this then turns into its successor, Gemini, a Mutable Sign of the Element Air.

Thus just as yang inevitably turns into yin at its height, and yin in its fullness dissolves into yang, so the continuous cycle of the moving principles turns from one Mode into another until all 12 Signs are completed. The first manifestation of this principle, the Cardinal, is initiatory, it thrusts its Sign out into the beginning towards a new way of functioning. Then it merges into a concentration of energy in the Fixed Signs. Finally it is dispersed out into the world according to its Mutable nature, and then the cycle begins again from a new beginning.

The second factor comprises the group of Sun, Moon, planets and Angles. I have said that when the Signs of the Zodiac are activated, their respective qualities are revealed. What does 'activated' mean? It means that the quality of a particular Sign will be brought out when, and for the period in which, one of the bodies just mentioned is in that Sign. These bodies therefore are like the hands of a clock and in the descriptive sense they act as the measurements of the quality of time.

Synesius of Cyrene, Bishop of Alexandria in the fifth century, said that history repeats itself because the stars return to their former positions. The time taken to return to their former positions, or to travel around the complete circle of the Zodiac depends on the distance of the planet from the earth. Pluto, at the farthest reaches of our solar system, takes a period of approximately 250 years, Neptune 165 years, Uranus 84 years, Saturn 29 years, Jupiter 12 years and Mars only two years. Venus and Mercury, from our geocentric vantage point, being between the earth and the Sun, are tied to the approximate time the Sun itself takes.

The Sun of course takes a year and its path creates the Signs of the Zodiac and the annual seasons. The Moon takes but a month and the motion of the earth itself, focused at the rising point or Ascendant, marks out a period of one day as it revolves on its axis. Thus the time that any of these bodies is in, or activates, a particular Sign will be for a twelfth of the total time taken to revolve round the complete band of the Zodiac.

Naturally all these bodies are moving round the Zodiac and so through the Signs continuously, and therefore there will be a constant interplay of activation by the different bodies for different periods of time. Here we find the differentiation between the ages. There is a generation backdrop of a certain quality when the slower moving planets inhabit a Sign which influences, in the case of Pluto and Neptune, a whole generation, right down to the passing hour it takes the Ascendant to sweep through a Sign.

The planets do not of course travel around the Zodiac independently. Although for convenience we look at them separately, in reality they form a constant interplay of movement which creates a changing relationship between each separate factor. This relationship comprises the third factor with which we have to deal, that of the aspects.

The effect of the aspects is to modify the underlying quality contained in the Signs. This modification takes place first, because the combination of different planets produces ease or difficulty in expressing the quality of the Signs, depending on the nature of those planets; second, because as the planets move closer into a meaningful relationship they produce a state of climax or crisis; and third, because they bring together the nature of the Signs in which the planets are placed at the time of the relevant aspect.

From the descriptive viewpoint the aspects are of the greatest importance and we shall see their practical application in Part Two. At this stage I want to look at the first two points I have just mentioned more closely. The third should be clear. First, modification of the quality of the Signs will be brought about according to the nature of the planets themselves, and this will affect the way that quality will be expressed. Thus the underlying quality of a two-and-a-half day period will be described by the Sign occupied by the Moon. If the Moon is in Aries this underlying quality will be outgoing, assertive, spontaneous, impetuous. Those qualities will then be modified according to the nature of any planet which aspects the Moon.

Pluto will produce tension, the threat of repressed forces coming to the surface, explosions, heaviness, thunder. Neptune introduces an element of the unworldly, whether of the spiritual or imaginative realms, or confusion, deceit, deviousness. Uranus magnetizes, electrifies, excites and breaks down like lightning.

Saturn frustrates in its slow determination, or reinforces concentration by steady application. It can be restrictive or it can enhance effective planning and aid long-term solutions. Jupiter exaggerates existing conditions, providing optimism and hope which may result in lack of judgement or open generosity. Mars is assertive and aggressive and speeds up the quality of the period, causing anger, irritation, impatience or dynamism and courage.

The second form of modification takes place because as the planets move closer into a meaningful relationship they produce a state of climax or crisis. Here we need to examine the term 'meaningful relationship' and then see how the state of crisis is reached. As the theory of harmonics has emphasized, in an absolute sense all the planets will always be in some form of aspect to each other because the circle of the Zodiac can be divided by any number. In practice, however, some aspects are meaningful in the sense that they are effective in electional astrology while others are not.

From this point of view elections is a branch of mundane astrology in that it is concerned with bringing things into manifestation and with what occurs in the world. And the aspects which are concerned with manifestation are those which are the result of dividing the circle by multiples of the number two. In practice the aspects that are relevant in elections are the major 'hard' aspects: the conjunction, square and opposition. It is these alone with which we have to deal.

A state of climax is reached because in elections we are dealing with movement. In natal astrology we interpret a frozen moment of time. If the Moon in a Natal Chart is at 5 degrees of Cancer and Saturn is at 8 degrees of Aries there is a square aspect between these two bodies. If Saturn is at 3 degrees of Aries there is still a square aspect between them and, apart from the potency of the distance between them, the meaning in terms of character is the same.

But in elections this is not so. Because the planets are in a continual state of movement there is constant change. We are not looking here at a frozen present but at the movement of time itself. The enterprise with which we are concerned is not just born in a moment. It lives on. And if we look at what happens in time we can see that things come to a climax and if we then look at an ephemeris of the planetary positions we can see that this climax correlates with the planetary aspects. As the planets move in the sky they constantly move towards each other, then they form an exact aspect, then they move away from it, and so on through another set of aspects.

The climax is reached when the planet is exactly in aspect. As it moves towards exactitude the power is increased. Once it has passed the exact aspect the effect is spent. So in elections the situation is very different from that in natal astrology. In the example I mentioned above, if Saturn were at 3 degrees of Aries it would be coming up to the aspect and would therefore be effective. At 5 degrees of Aries the aspect would be exact and therefore its potency would be at its height. As soon as Saturn has gone beyond that point its effect is over.

Where the Moon is being aspected the effects can be felt a day before exactitude. To return to the example of the Moon activating the Sign of Aries, if Pluto is coming up to an opposition with the Moon, tension will build up as the aspect approaches during the day before exactitude. The climax will occur when the aspect is exact in terms of Pluto's nature and the Sign of Aries and then the situation will subside. The interplay of these forces is a sacred drama of circumstances, as conflict heightens towards its inevitable resolution in crisis, with its resolution at the climax, its descent following fulfilment, until the conflict builds up again towards the next crisis and resolution.

In practice it is likely that more than one planet will be forming an aspect. Two planets may be in conjunction, so both will form an aspect with a third. Or two may be in hard aspect with each other. So, if Mars and Jupiter are themselves in square aspect, when Mars forms an opposition to the Moon, Jupiter will form a square aspect to the Moon.

The fourth and final factor is the diurnal cycle, or the motion of the earth itself. The relevance of this factor is twofold. We have already seen that the Angles, effectively as focussed in the Ascendant, form one of the measurements of time in the same way as the Sun, Moon and planets. So when the Ascendant is in a particular Sign that Sign will be activated for a period of approximately two hours.

The Angles and Houses also ground the enterprise and show where on the mundane level the various principles will be effective and how they are placed in those areas. Here we go from the general to the particular. How important this is in practice will depend on the nature of the particular enterprise. If we are selecting a time for a marriage, for example, then factors in the 3rd House will show the situation with regard to brothers and sisters on this mundane level. I have discussed these four factors in the order they should be chosen as we shall see when we put theory into practice in the second half of this book. First, we choose the underlying quality of the time for the enterprise depending on the nature of that enterprise by looking at the Signs of the Zodiac. Second, a decision must be made as to the duration of that quality when we look at the Sun, Moon, planets and Ascendant. Third, we both choose certain qualities and avoid others by taking account of the combination of the planets in the aspects. Finally, we take account, if relevant, of the specific areas on the mundane level which are applicable in the Houses.

One glory of the Sun: astrology, the time element of magic

There is one glory of the Sun, and another of the Moon, and another glory of the stars: for one star differeth from another in glory.

1 Corinthians[5]

In this section I shall examine the cyclic approach to time. Cyclic time rests on the premise that every principle in the universe develops according to its own pattern in time. We live in the phenomenal world. We see nations, peoples, natural disasters, trends in music and literature, religious revivals and scientific discovery. Each has its distinct pattern in time, rising and falling over centuries and generations.

These patterns can be studied independently. Meteorologists examine variations in the weather to predict floods, frost, hailstorms or hurricanes. Economists look at the changing rhythms of the stock markets while demographers note the periodic recurrences of shifting populations. Looking at the occurrence of events on their own is the approach of the materialist who is only concerned with the mundane level of existence.

If, however, we look beyond the particular to the general it is possible to see that the manifestation of events on earth is only the material expression of principles which are universal. These principles operate behind the manifestation in the phenomenal world and are reflected in the heavenly bodies. By examining the cycles of the Sun, Moon and planets directly we can see the pattern of the archetypal principles which govern events on earth.

The archetypal principles operate on all levels. The principles themselves are those which form the universe in every aspect of its existence – from God at its highest level to the earth at its lowest and with man stretched between the two. When the universe was recognized to be a unity the universal principles which lay behind existence were symbolized by the 10 numbers, or sephiroth, in the system of the Tree of Life in the Kabbalah. This system of knowledge was the basis of magic, the understanding of the laws of the universe which was generally accepted before the rise of materialistic science separated material phenomena from archetypal principles.

The archetypal principles, or sephiroth, on the Tree of Life are static. They form the blueprint of existence representing the ideal state, of God, the world, of man and all other forms of existence. These 10 sephiroth are represented by the Sun, Moon and planets which move in time through their recurring cycles producing the pattern of life. Astrology is therefore the time element of magic.

The aim of the magician was to bring about change on earth. The way to do this was to arrange things so that heaven and earth were in harmony. It was accepted that not only was there a right state for each principle but that there was also a right time for every purpose under heaven. In order to find the right time for his purpose, the magician studied the cycles of the planets and chose the appropriate part of the cycle of the planet which governed his enterprise.

The same holds true today. The principles which govern the universe have not altered even though much of the terminology inevitably sounds archaic. To find the correct part of the planetary cycle it is necessary first to know which principle governs which kind of enterprise, and second, how the planetary cycles operate.

With these precepts in mind, we can examine the ingredients of cyclic time. These are: first, the planets, including here the Sun and Moon; second, the Signs of the Zodiac; third, the phases of the planets, including the Moon; and fourth, the planetary days and hours. As we have seen, the archetypal principles which govern every facet of the universe at every level are symbolized by the planets. Finding the right part of their cycles means placing them in the appropriate degree, and Sign, of the Zodiac, while their effects will be modified according to their phase and refined, if necessary, in the planetary days and hours.

The first factor comprises the Sun, Moon and planets. It is these which symbolize the archetypal principles. The principles symbolized by the planets operate down through the levels of manifestation until they materialize in events on earth. The first step, according to this system, is to find the planet which governs the enterprise and in order to do this it is necessary to be aware of the principle behind the enterprise.

Recognizing the true principle may not always be a simple matter. If, for example, the election concerns the foundation of a university then it may be assumed that the principle of learning is that which governs the enterprise, in which case Mercury would be chosen as the appropriate planet. On the other hand, the project may be seen as the expression of the institution itself and in this event Jupiter would be the natural choice.

As we shall see in Part Two when we come to formulate the rules, the possibility of an enterprise being governed by more than one principle will not be mutually exclusive in terms of the planetary cycles. In the example of a university it would be possible to choose the appropriate part of the cycles of both planets. However, when it comes to refining the overall position in terms of planetary contacts and the diurnal cycle, conflicting rules may operate.

In practice, recognizing the planet which governs the principle of the enterprise has not been the main problem. The real problem has taken place before that stage has been reached. As I have stressed throughout this book, elections are concerned first and foremost with the enterprise itself. That being so the planetary principle which must always be considered is that which governs the enterprise. What has unfortunately happened is that, on the analogy of natal and horary astrology, an Ascendant has been chosen and then the planet ruling that Ascendant is assumed to govern the enterprise. It is this situation which has led to the confusion of the real principles of electional astrology.

For practical and historical reasons the planetary principles begin with Saturn at the farthest limits. For historical reasons this is so because the three outer planets, Uranus, Neptune and Pluto, were only discovered comparatively recently. That in itself would not preclude the use of these bodies. But practical reasons make it unlikely that the outer planets could be used in the time-span available for a meaningful choice, bearing in mind that Uranus takes 84 years to complete its cycle round the Zodiac while Pluto takes approximately 250 years.

Let us then look at the principles symbolized by the planets. In looking at these it is in general terms important to appreciate that the manifestation of any principle will be revealed at different levels on a hierarchical basis. Thus, having established the archetypal essence of the principle, the possibilities can be established from the abstract to the material, through the spectrum of different levels incorporating the intuitive, the intellectual, the volitional, the emotional to the physical.

The archetypal principle of Saturn is structure and order. This will manifest in terms of discipline, limitation, restriction and produce stability and endurance. Its principle will be found in authority and tradition, in prisons, hospitals, among the police and the more restraining aspects of government. It will also be found in old age and in death, in material things, especially in the land, in agriculture and farming.

Jupiter, by way of contrast, is concerned with expansion, growth, abundance and plenty. Its principle is co-operation, the dreams and vision of the higher mind and spirituality and the results can be seen in social institutions, philosophy, and publishing, as well as in material growth and physical exuberance. While Jupiter binds together and produces solidarity, Mars divides and separates. It is the assertive force of conquest and will-power, creating and destroying by its individuality and drive. It materializes in the armed forces, in surgery and sport.

The principle of Venus is harmony – in its highest form, love. It attracts to itself either selflessly through devotion, creatively through art, beauty and entertainment, or materially through self-indulgence, luxury and financial affluence. Mercury governs communication, self-expression through words, speech and writing. In the material world it finds expression through commerce, education and travel.

I have left the Sun and Moon until last as their role is a dual one. First, they represent archetypal principles like the planets. Thus, the principle of the Sun is honour and leadership. It governs success, in material terms, superiors, employers, power and, on the physical level, health. The principle of the Moon is change, the fluctuations of life as a whole which manifest in mundane affairs, in the people and especially in relation to women.

The second role of these two bodies is a more general one. The Sun and the Moon represent the two polar forces upon which the universe exists, the yang and the yin. Esoterically the Sun represents the spirit and the Moon the soul and because of their general application they focus the principles of the planets on earth. Acting in the form of the god and the goddess, the seasons of the former and the phases of the latter have always been of prime importance in the choice of time for magical ritual, much of which has now been assimilated by Christianity in its recognition of the natural cycles of these heavenly forces.

We have established that the aim in the cyclic approach is to ensure that the planets are in the right part of their cycles. These cycles are the Signs of the Zodiac which comprise the second factor from this perspective. The meaning of the Signs of the Zodiac is the same in both the descriptive and the cyclic systems. They provide the underlying quality of time. The difference between the two systems lies in the way the planets bring out this quality.

In the descriptive system the planets act as the measurements of time. So we choose the quality which is appropriate according to the Sign and the duration of that quality according to the planet. In the cyclic system we decide which planet governs the enterprise and then choose the quality of time according to the Signs because that quality is right according to the inherent cycle of the particular planet.

The affinity between the planets and the Signs is based on three principles. First, there is a general sympathy between certain planets and certain areas of the Zodiac and correspondingly there are general areas in the Zodiac where each planet functions least effectively. Each planet has its greatest general affinity in the degree and, to a lesser extent, in the Sign of its exaltation. The opposite degree, and to the same extent the Sign, is its fall, and is the least favourable part of its cycle.

After the exaltation comes the rulership. In that degree, and Sign, a planet will find its next most favourable area. Correspondingly, the opposite part of the cycle, its detriment, will be the second least favourable area. Then a planet will be more compatible in certain Signs than in others. Mars, as an assertive, outgoing planet will in general function best in the Fire Signs, while it will function less effectively in the Water Signs. A full list of these degrees and Signs,

The Signs	Planetary exaltation	Degree of exaltation	Planetary fall	Rulership (yang +, yin −)	Detriment
ARIES	Sun	19	Saturn	Mars +	Venus
TAURUS	Moon	3		Venus −	Mars Pluto
GEMINI				Mercury +	Jupiter
CANCER	Jupiter	15	Mars	Moon	Saturn
LEO				Sun	Saturn Uranus
VIRGO	Mercury	15	Venus	Mercury −	Jupiter Neptune
LIBRA	Saturn	21	Sun	Venus +	Mars
SCORPIO			Moon	Mars − Pluto	Venus
SAGITTARIUS				Jupiter +	Mercury
CAPRICORN	Mars	28	Jupiter	Saturn −	Moon
AQUARIUS				Saturn + Uranus	Sun
PISCES	Venus	27	Mercury	Jupiter − Neptune	Mercury

Table 3.1 List of Signs and degrees in order of compatibility

in the order of their compatibility, will be found in Table 3.1.

Although these terms sound archaic, the principle behind them is sound. Just as individual lives rise and fall at certain times, one man's fame flourishing at 30 while another's genius is protracted until 50, and a third's disgrace falls at 40, so the individual planetary principles peak and trough at certain times in their cycles. The use of the old terms suggests an emphasis on the space element of the Zodiac, whereas if we keep in mind the conceptual movement of the planets through the Signs, we realize that time and space blend into one dimension.

The second principle is based on the fact that each planet (and for this purpose the Sun and Moon are together regarded as one body) rules, or functions appropriately in, two Signs, one yang and one yin. This dual rulership is generally regarded today as of no more than historical interest because the original principle behind the rulerships has been forgotten.

However, in electional astrology the principle is of vital importance. The zodiacal cycle, as we saw in the last section, is divided by the first three numbers and this division creates the polarities, the Elements and the Modes. Here we are concerned with the division into the two basic directions of energy, the yang and the yin, the active and receptive, which form the essence of all life and motion in the universe.

I made the point earlier that astrology was originally the time element of magic. The first rule in magical ceremonies was to decide on the intent. If the intent was to give, then the appropriate energy was the yang or the outgoing. If, on the other hand, the intent was to get something, then the appropriate energy was the yin or receptive. Similarly there was a yang and yin colour which corresponded to each planetary energy.

Thus the second matter is to decide whether the purpose of the enterprise is to give or to receive. If the intention is to give, the appropriate planet should be placed in its yang Sign, whereas if it is to receive, it should be placed in its yin Sign. So if the enterprise is concerned with love and the intention is to give love to another, Venus will be placed in its yang Sign, Libra. On the other hand, if the enterprise is concerned with obtaining love from another, Venus will be placed in its yin Sign, Taurus. The reason why the Sun and Moon 'rule' only one Sign each is that the Sun represents the yang force itself and the Moon the yin. Thus the purpose of the solar power will always be to pour its strength out, while that of the lunar force will be to attract and draw inwards.

These two principles are concerned with the general correlation of the planets with the Signs. The third concerns the particular purpose of the enterprise. The most appropriate place in general for Mars is the degree of its exaltation, 28 degrees of Capricorn, but if we are concerned with the foundation of a centre for water sports then Mars, which governs sports, would be more appropriately placed in the opposite Sign, Cancer. In this example, the two principles, the general and the particular, are diametrically opposed and it is here especially that judgement needs to be exercised in making a specific choice.

The third factor in the cyclic approach is analogous to the aspects in the descriptive system but there is a difference in emphasis. In the cyclic approach we are concerned with the phases of the planets and especially of the Moon. The disparity between phases and aspects lies in their duration. A phase lasts for a quarter of the total cycle, or from one hard aspect to the next. In practice the phases of the planets are of little importance. The phases which do have great effect are those of the Moon which combine the potency of both the Sun and the Moon in the latter.

The fourth, and final, factor is the system of planetary days and hours. Here we have what appears to be a total divergence from the descriptive approach. Just as the planets rule, or are more appropriate in, different periods of time through the Signs of the Zodiac, so they rule certain days of the week and certain hours of the day and night. For example, if we are concerned with an enterprise relating to honour, the most appropriate day and hour will be those ruled by the Sun. Although the effect of choosing the day and the hour according to their planetary rulerships is different from the practice of choosing the time of day according to the descriptive quality of the Ascendant, nevertheless the principle behind both systems is the same in so far as they provide a more exact time by invoking the diurnal cycles.

The electional horoscope: a composition in time

The purpose of this chapter has been to understand the nature of time in so far as it is relevant to electional astrology. If we are to create an electional horoscope, which means choosing the time that is right for an enterprise, we must first understand the nature of time. We must also understand the ingredients of time and know how they correlate with the factors that are the symbols of astrology.

We have looked at time from two perspectives, from the descriptive and the cyclic. Yet it is clear that what we are looking at is the same. The factors themselves are for the most part identical – the planets, the Signs of the Zodiac, the relationship between the planets, whether we call them aspects or phases. Although we are not specifically concerned with the Houses in the cyclic view nor with the planetary houses in the descriptive, we are merely ignoring elements that exist because they are not relevant according to our particular frame of reference.

Astrology in general is a symbolic way of understanding reality. Understanding implies perceiving and naturally what we perceive depends on what we are trying to understand. If we are trying to understand a static situation, a time divorced from past and future, of anything born in a particular moment of time, whether human or inanimate, then we look at that one moment of time, cut off from its past and separated from its prospective future. And this then is how we will perceive that time because that is the reality with which we are concerned.

So natal astrology is descriptive. Here we are concerned only with the quality of the moment. We look at the Sun in Leo and interpret that fixed phenomenon. We stop there and in stopping there we stop the Sun in Leo. Mundane astrology, to take another branch of the art, is cyclic. Here we are concerned with the rise and fall of nations, institutions, the pattern of war and peace, of economies, of trade and learning. And so here we look at the moving cycles of the planets through the Signs of the Zodiac, weaving their web of existence through time.

We have two perspectives therefore because we are trying to see two things. And in doing so we need to appreciate both the duality and the unity of time. Certainly logic should deny the conclusion that just because we are seeing two things there must be two different kinds of time in an objective sense. Nevertheless the conclusion that there is no difference between the two perceptions would be equally false.

Originally, when astrology was used in a different way, when man's perception of reality was more united, and when astrology and magic were accepted as two parts of one system, the split was not so apparent, if indeed it existed at all. Now that the magic has gone out of the world, it is difficult for the majority of people to recapture its spirit. But whether we realize it or not we are part of a magical universe.

Even though we no longer accept the path of the Sun as the god's journey through the world each year, and even though we do not recognize the Moon's path each month as the way of the goddess, we cannot entirely extinguish their lights. The festivals, the seasons, the sacrifices and even the glimmerings of faith exist in their outward

form in modern religious guise, dedicated to the real power of the
god and the goddess though we are no longer in touch with their
spirit.

Let us examine each perspective in turn to find the common ground
upon which both rest. If we look at time from the descriptive
viewpoint, we see a time when Mars is in Gemini. During this two-
month period the principle of communication will be in operation
through people, ideas and transport. When we look at the aspects
we see how this underlying principle is affected by the principles
symbolized by the other planets; communication is restricted by
Saturn, magnetized by Uranus, delayed by Neptune, threatened by
Pluto, or expanded by Jupiter.

Now if we turn to the cyclic perspective, we see that Mars represents
the principle of assertiveness. When Mars moves through Gemini,
transport speeds up, links are forged between nations, ideas are
expressed forcibly, and there is danger of disruption in travel, perhaps
manifesting in a series of accidents in the air depending on the other
factors in operation.

What then is the principle that unites the two systems? It is that
each principle has its individual cycle and this cycle lasts for the period
which the body representing that principle takes to complete one
circuit of the Zodiac. Mars, therefore, symbolizing assertiveness, has
a two-year cycle. In the course of that two-year period it describes
each of the 12 underlying qualities in turn. In the same way the
principle of honour and glory, symbolized by the Sun, has an annual
cycle, while the principle of order and structure, symbolized by
Saturn, has a cycle of approximately 29 years. Each principle therefore
lives in time and is an element of time.

From a practical point of view it is important to appreciate both
the unity and the divergence of the two systems for in practice what
we are trying to achieve in a particular election will vary. In every
case we shall be trying to get the planets into the right area of the
Zodiac. But what is the right area will depend on the particular
purpose of the enterprise. So if we are primarily concerned with
getting the right time for a particular energy we should look at the
cycles of the planets, while if our primary aim is to choose a particular
quality, we should concentrate on the descriptive approach.

The reality, in an objective sense, is the same. The planets are in
the Signs. The planets move through the Signs. It is as valid to say
that they are in the Signs as that they move through the Signs. Our
perception depends on what we want to see. If we are concerned
with description then we look at Mars in Gemini. It will be that kind

of time and we can choose that specific quality of time for our enterprise. Yet Mars moves through Gemini. The quality of the Signs themselves, in themselves separate, changes as life itself changes.

It is this change which produces the cyclic, or magical, perception. Here we start with the body that governs the enterprise and then see when it will reach the area of the Zodiac which is most appropriate for the enterprise. In this cyclic viewpoint we leave the static perception of description and move towards a dramatic view of reality. The forces of the universe, personified by the gods and goddesses in the form of the planets, move in conflict, climax and resolution, in life, death and rebirth, to form the sacred drama of life.

By being in touch with the quality of time, recognizing the different qualities that occur, seeing precisely when these qualities are brought into manifestation, when the crises approach, when they climax, when they fall away to rise again, we are also in touch with the underlying pattern, with the cyclic nature of time which circles the world like Jormungand. The two blend into the one they always were but in remaining in touch with these two separate views of reality we come to realize that:

The causes are in time; only their issue
Is bodied in the flesh, the finite powers.

4.

THE TAO OF HEAVEN:
TIME IN THE EAST

In the last chapter we saw that the quality of time changes, from generation to generation, as from moment to moment. In this chapter we shall see how change as a principle is incorporated in time and get a deeper understanding of the meaning of time and its place in electional astrology.

In order to get this deeper understanding we need to shift our perception. Picasso tells the story of how he would hang his paintings upside down so that he could see the fundamental shapes and lines of the pictures without being encumbered by their pictorial representations. Time is a strange phenomenon because although it never ceases to move we have come to perceive it as a series of separate moments.

This tendency is emphasized in astrology. Astrology is the science of time but its time is an artificial one for we look at moments and we break up the continuous stream of existence. In its way this is as right as it is natural and to a great extent it is a part of our Western heritage. But in elections we enter into a wider dimension of time, time as a continual process of change. In order to appreciate this dimension we shall in this chapter move to the Eastern viewpoint of time before returning to our own Western perspective in Chapter 5.

All life is change. In the West we think of change as something happening to us. We see change in the seasons as summer turns to autumn, and winter into spring. We see it in the Signs of the Zodiac when Aries is followed by Taurus and Taurus gives way to Gemini. We see it too in the continual movement of the heavenly bodies, and in our own physical bodies – the baby growing into youth, from maturity to old age, from wisdom to senility.

But there is another way of seeing change. This kind of change is inherent in every aspect of the universe, and in every part of it reflected in the symbols of astrology. One thing does not just change into another. That other is inherent in its inception and is but another aspect of its being. The old man looks out from the baby's eyes just as spring has germinated in the depths of winter. By looking through the present the future can be glimpsed, for beneath the surface the two are one. Every moment, every note of stillness in the universe, is changing. Aries does not just give way to the appearance of Taurus; the latter is a part of the former as both are parts of a whole process.

Used as we are to looking at things separately, it is not easy to suspend old habits and see the world in a new and fresher way. Nevertheless it is important to learn to see the heavenly bodies which are astrology's symbols as a continual process of change. Not only will this viewpoint enable us to understand the wider potentials of elections but it will enrich our lives by enabling us to accept the changes that are our own destiny.

In natal astrology we stop the heavens and dissect one moment of time; in effect we are looking at one single frame of a moving film. So we forget that in reality the moment never stops. In electional astrology, however, we are not just looking at a frozen moment of time. The difference is important for two reasons. The first is because we are choosing not only the moment but the future of that moment. If, for example, we are choosing a time for a business venture, we will be concerned not only with the business itself as an independent entity but also with the future of the enterprise. In natal astrology we can only interpret the future which is inherent in the present, but in elections we can choose both.

The second reason is because change governs the nature of time itself. The moment of time is not only a moment but an aspect of time in its entirety. Each moment, each part of the cycle, is made up of the interaction of different forces which show how the direction of time will be fulfilled. Again, through Western eyes, we see things as parts of a static present. This tendency is apparent, for instance, when we look at the Moon's phases or the seasons of the Sun.

To us the Full Moon represents the opposition, one of the hard aspects between the Sun and the Moon. But in the fullness of its power, at the very height of the solar potency, lightening the darkest night, it spills out into its opposite and begins the waning cycle of the lunar force. All things are connected. This inbeing changes not only the future but the nature and meaning of the Full Moon itself for its future exists before the present was born.

This brings us to the very heart of astrology where future and present blend into one and where we are as able to see the unfolding of time in the moment as we can see death in a young man's face. So in order to understand the inner dimension of time which incorporates the dynamic aspect of change, we need to see the changes at work through time.

Specifically we need to shift our viewpoint from the static perception of the West, where Aries is Aries and Taurus is only Taurus, to a more fluid and a more interrelated perception of time. It is this inner dynamic, the moving face of time, that can be seen in the Eastern viewpoint which we shall now describe.

The Eastern concept of time: balance and continuity

In movement benevolence shows itself in timing.

Lao Tzu (*Tao-te-Ching*)[1]

Balance is the goal of Chinese philosophy, a balance between the two forces in the universe that together make up the whole. This balance can only be reached by the acceptance of the continual changes that exist in the world. The pattern of change in China is illustrated in the great work of the *I Ching*, the *Book of Changes*.

Time, as an aspect of nature, is change, and change, as an aspect of time, is of two kinds, although the two are one. The one is the Tao and is time as a whole, or eternity. The time that we see at work in our daily lives is the T'ai I, the Great Changer, that exists within the Tao and this consists of the continual interplay of the ying and the yang.

Understanding time in the East, then, consists to a large extent of understanding the relationship between the Tao, on the one hand, and the T'ai I, on the other. Chinese culture is essentially poetic, the pictures used to describe their ideas being more graphic than rational. Let us then start with this description of the Tao:

The Tao is a softly lucent ocean of pure void, a pearly mist, boundless, immaculate. Born of this ocean, two dragons sport entwined – the male, bright as the Sun with fiery golden scales, master of activity; the female, radiant as the Moon with shining silver scales, adept at passivity. Their intercourse brings forth the rhythms of cyclic change – the movements of the planets, the progression of the seasons, the alternation of day and night.[2]

The Tao is made up of the unending flux of time as the ocean is made up of the unceasing ebb and flow of the tides and the continuous currents that exist within it. The Tao is structure and the yang and yin form the changes that take place within that structure. But although the Tao is therefore in unending flux, being in unceasing change from moment to moment, the changes themselves proceed in orderly cycles, each pattern being endlessly repeated and therefore these changes form the structure of the whole.

This realization was derived from the observation of nature's cyclic patterns which could be seen in the movements of the planetary bodies as in all aspects of life and in their interpretation in terms of yang and yin. This realization is now also accepted among quantum physicists who have appreciated that the structure which appears on the surface of physical reality is in fact made up of continuous change on the quantum level.

The changes themselves consist of the interplay between the two opposing forces – the yang and the yin. The yang is the master of activity, the male dragon bright as the Sun, while the yin is the female dragon, adept at passivity, radiant as the Moon. Once again, if we look at these forces visually we can see how, although opposites, they encompass each other and how, at their extreme, they turn into each other. Thus the yang is a continuous line. Now the nature of the yang is active and this trait, carried to its extreme, will produce a tension which results in the line being broken – into two smaller lines, forming the yin. Equally, the yin, whose nature is receptive, moves inward and, carried to its extreme, will coalesce – to form a continuous line, the yang. We can see this process illustrated in Fig. 4.1.

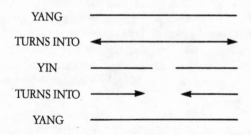

Figure 4.1 The yang and yin lines

The natural order of things can be seen in the constant interplay between these two forces which form their patterns in time and space. At one time the yang force will be in the ascendant, while at another the yin will prevail. At certain times then the yang will be at its height, while at others the yin will reach its maximum force. At times the two principles will be equal, in a state of balance. But none of these times can last; the pattern inevitably changes and repeats itself.

As we watch this continual interplay we see the difference in the Eastern and Western viewpoints. In the East the view is that there is no good and evil such as is accepted in the West; on the contrary the only evil is seen as excess and that is why it is necessary for the individual to align himself with the total pattern which contains both yang and yin, knowing that the one will soon pass into the other. In the West, on the contrary, the tendency is to regard the opposites as confronting each other. The aim is also balance, but here it is the balance of containing the two opposing forces instead of regarding them as aspects of each other.

Hence we see the old distinction between benefic, 'good', planets, notably Jupiter and Venus, and malefic, or 'bad' ones, notably Saturn and Mars. And even though we now more commonly regard these forces as neutral they are still conceived of as separate energies confronting each other. The archetypal symbolism of the planetary energies on the Tree of Life in the system of the Kabbalah makes this apparent, with the principles of change and structure themselves opposing each other at the top of the two pillars in the form of Chokmah and Binah.[3]

As the opposites are contained in each other, the Chinese realized that excessive 'good' would inevitably lead to 'evil' and indeed that 'evil' was nature's attempt to restore the balance. The role of the emperor, the 'Son of Heaven', consisted of putting the universe in harmony with the celestial order and maintaining an uneasy balance between extremes, rather like a man riding a bicycle, continually in motion with one foot up and the other down. Or, to use a favourite Chinese analogy, rowing a boat with the two oars in perfect equilibrium. But balance itself should not be excessive or it will lead to stagnation, as we can see from the bicyclist who would fall off if he kept still.

The interchange between time as a whole and the moving patterns which form the overall structure are encompassed in the language, as in the hexagrams of the *I Ching*. The latter, as they relate specifically to time and the seasons, will be examined in the next section. Here we can mention the different layers of meaning which are contained in the title and which illustrate beautifully the principle of opposites contained in each other.

According to Richard Wilhelm 'I' originally meant lizard and in particular the chameleon. As he says: 'The name *I* has three meanings.

These are the easy, the changing and the constant.'[4] On the one hand there is the idea of changeability, easy mobility, that which happens effortlessly; while at the other extreme there is the concept of command, that which is granted by a feudal lord to his vassal, or the fixed relationship between lord and vassal. Here we have the inclusive concept of freedom and structure mentioned above which co-exists just as time co-exists with eternity.

The freedom that is change, the natural movement of things within pre-existing relationships, follows a definite pattern. The changing laws of the universe, taken together, comprise the law itself, the T'ai I within the Tao. So we find three kinds of change. First, there is cyclical change where one thing changes into another but in the course of that change the original thing is restored. Examples of this phenomenon are the seasons and the phases of the Moon.

Second, there is progressive development or evolution. Here one state of things progressively changes into another, but in this case the original thing does not revert into its initial condition. An example of this kind of change is old age and the days of a man's life where each day contains the sum total of his preceding days.

Third, there is the immutable law that works through all transformation, the principle of the creative, the active force which endures through time. Here both kinds of time, change and eternity, are combined. It is here that we find the great polarity of the Tai Chi, the unity behind duality, the root of all changes, the Tao behind the yang-yin. Thus total change, the complete cycle, is structure, the law, or wholeness, the Tao itself.

The combination of the yang and the yin provides the whole essence of life according to the Chinese viewpoint. These combinations form the trigrams of the *I Ching* which contain the energies of the universe and of life; how they are mixed determines one's destiny. Because, according to this viewpoint, space and time are the same, each situation, as contained in the hexagrams, is both a moment in time and part of the continuous movement of time as a whole. Thus where one is at the time shows how the situation will evolve.

So what we in the West think of as a static situation is in fact also an aspect of the time cycle which is life. In the West, therefore, we separate space and time, while in the East the two are combined. Thus in Western Astrology, transits are separate from the birth chart, while in the East, all is contained in the changes that are reflected in the hexagrams. The election horoscope should combine both, and in practice this means adopting the Eastern perspective in order to see time as a moving pattern, the motion of the planets in their spheres.

The seasons in the East

The general principles of change that we have discussed are embodied in time. By looking at the seasons in the East we get a clear idea of the continual ebb and flow of time throughout the year. Here we can see how the quality of time correlates with the waxing and waning of the yang and yin forces. These annual phases are much like the monthly phases of the Moon when the dark New Moon is gradually filled with the yang solar power until it shines at its peak with the brilliance of the Full Moon. And then as soon as the power is at its height it begins to wane and the dark fills its surface.

The interplay of yang and yin, of light and dark, Sun and Moon, male and female, active and receptive, the golden and silver dragons or the Green Dragon and the White Tiger, have been seen in all periods of time, as much in day and night, in the lunar phases as in the annual cycle of the seasons. As the yang power increases so does the active force in the universe as a whole. Then it is the time for activity, for doing and pursuing, for achieving and sending forth. While the yin principle holds sway, the receptive energies of the universe are potent. Then it is time to reap and for drawing in, for wisdom and receiving.

The seasons are part of a continuous cycle when the yang and the yin rise and fall alternately, a gradual process of mingling, rather than separate periods as they are regarded in the West. We can see this clearly in Fig. 4.2 and 4.3. In Fig. 4.2 the seasons are shown in terms of the yang and yin forces in a linear way.

At the winter solstice there is pure yin with six broken lines. Then gradually the yang force emerges at the bottom, still overshadowed by the yin but nonetheless rising like ink on blotting paper, gradually spreading upwards. If we bear in mind what I said about the yang and the yin in the last section we shall recall that the opposites are contained in each other. So we should not think of the yang force coming from outside, but rather as evolving from the yin.

The point here is that, having reached its height, the yin must turn into its opposite. For the nature of the yin itself is receptive and therefore it turns into itself, and as it does so it consolidates and forms the continuous line of the yang. Throughout the winter the yin is more powerful than the yang but slowly the yang rises higher and higher until, at the spring equinox, the two are equal. At this moment in time there is balance; the boat as it were has stopped,

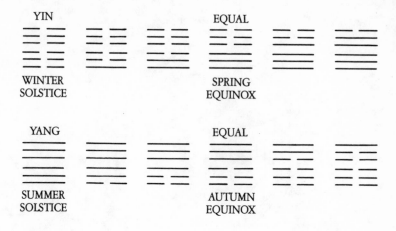

Figure 4.2 The seasons in the East – a linear view

both oars in the air. Then the moment is past; the oars pull once more and the boat moves on, never having stopped at all.

Throughout the spring the yang force rises higher and higher, as the days get longer and the sun hotter until at the summer solstice the earth is flooded with the solar power. Then for another moment of stillness the Green Dragon reigns supreme. This moment of time too breaks down as the yin force begins to rise. And here too we recall that the yin is contained in the yang for it is in the nature of the yang to expand and in doing so it breaks into two, forming the yin.

Even as summer begins, at the very height of the solar power, the days get shorter and the nights longer until at the autumn equinox balance is once more restored, with yin and yang, day and night, equal. Then the yin rises again and takes possession of time until once more winter calls. By looking at the seasons in this way we can see movement, not only throughout the year but in the lines themselves as one changes into another.

If we look now at Fig. 4.3 we see the same situation but this time instead of following a linear pattern we have the seasons arranged in a circle. It is easier here to see the seasons as opposites as well as the complete cycle and we can also see the correspondence between the areas and the Elements which were important in Chinese astrology and which we shall now look at in more detail.

The Chinese recognized the importance of descriptive as well as

YANG
SUMMER
FIRE
SOUTH

EAST
WOOD
SPRING

WEST
METAL
AUTUMN

NORTH
WATER
WINTER
YIN

Figure 4.3 The seasons in the East – a circular view

cyclic time. The seasons which we have just examined can be taken as the prime example of looking at the cyclic pattern of time in terms of the Sun, the annual ebb and flow of the two major powers that form the universe and its time element.

So they realized that if they wanted a particular enterprise to succeed they must begin when the compatible energies were right. In order to know when the energies were right for a particular enterprise they worked out a careful set of correspondences based on the Wu Hsing, the five Activities, or 'Elements'. These Activities are in themselves a breakdown of the original yang-yin duality as can be seen from Fig. 4.3 and as indeed our own four Elements are, the yang Elements in the West being Fire and Air, and the yin Elements Water and Earth. The difference in China is that the Centre is also classed as an Activity, although it functions too as the reconciliation of the other four Activities.

At the basis of this system was the idea that the workings of nature depend on an arrangement of fine balances among the various processes that may help, hinder or block one another according to the relative strength of each in a given situation. This knowledge could then be used to understand the workings of change in the universe. So if the enterprise were to wage war, the Activity would be Fire and the right season would be summer, the planet would be Mars, the Signs of the Zodiac Virgo and Libra and the time between 9 a.m. and 1 p.m. A full list of the Wu Hsing correspondences is given in Table 4.1.

Activity	wood	fire	earth	metal	water
Direction	east	south	centre	west	north
Colour	blue/green	red	yellow	white	black
Numbers	8 and 3	2 and 7	10 and 5	4 and 9	6 and 1
Climate	windy	hot	wet	dry	cold
Planet	Jupiter	Mars	Saturn	Venus	Mercury
Sound	shouting	laughing	singing	weeping	groaning
Virtue	benevolence	propriety	faith	rectitude	wisdom
Emotion	anger	joy	sympathy	grief	fear
Hour	3–7 a.m.	9 a.m.–1 p.m.	1–3 a.m., 7–9 a.m., 7–9 p.m.	3–7 p.m.	9 p.m.–1 a.m.
CELESTIAL STEM:					
Yin	i	ting	chi	hsin	kuei
Yang	chia	ping	wu	keng	jen
TERRESTIAL BRANCH:					
	yin, mao	ssu, wu	ch'ou, wei ch'en, hsu	shen, yu	tzu, hai
Zodiac	Gemini Cancer	Virgo Libra	Taurus Leo Scorpio Aquarius	Sagittarius Capricorn	Aries Pisces
Animal	dragon	phoenix	ox	tiger	snake tortoise

Table 4.1 The Wu Hsing correspondences

The Chinese were also aware of the part the individual must play in his enterprises, and they recognized the difference between the individual on the one hand and the enterprise on the other. Thus the emphasis was very different from that in the West which led to the enterprise being attached to the individual rather than the other way round. In China it was correctly recognized that if the enterprise were to succeed the time must be right for that enterprise. It was then a question of aligning the individual to the enterprise rather than the enterprise to the individual.

Deciding whether the enterprise was right for the individual meant

comparing the time of the enterprise with the horoscope of the
individual. In doing so it may have been discovered that the
individual should not be involved in that kind of enterprise in the
first place. Thus if the issue was when should X wage war, an
appropriate time would first be chosen for waging war. Then the
astrologer would look at X's horoscope to see if he should wage war,
and only then would he decide whether it would be right for him
to wage war at the chosen time.

As one Chinese master put it when asked whether a magistrate
named Chin should undertake a particular enterprise: 'A sage would
have succeeded where Chin failed, simply because it was in his nature
to fail, just as it is in the nature of a sage to succeed in everything
by going along with things instead of trying to overcome them.
Nature, you will find, takes her course whether men say yea or
nay.'5

5.

THE WHEEL OF FORTUNE: TIME IN THE WEST

The Western concept of time: crisis and change

> Gods may stay in mid-heaven, the son of man has
>   climbed to the Whitsun zenith,
> But I, Matthew, being a man
> Am a traveller back and forth.
>
> D.H. Lawrence (St Matthew)

The stillness of time is eternity. In the West we stop time to see it the better. But time for us is motion. Being men we travel back and forth while the gods are still. Being men too without a vantage point we often fail to see the coming hour as we miss the passing moment.

As we look at time through Western eyes, comparing and combining our perception with that of the East, we should develop an understanding of the nature of time which is central to electional astrology. To gain this understanding we should appreciate two preliminary points. The first is the natural tendency to see time as a series of separate moments just as we tend to see life as a series of isolated incidents. The second is the assumption that the nature of time is created only as a result of one force acting upon another.

Let us look at these two points in turn. The first is a matter of perception. Joshua made the Sun stand still. We, too, make time stand still in order to look at it. In doing so we forget that the moment of time is no more than a convenient, and artifical, way of looking at something that is in continual motion. By stopping the film we turn it into a series of separate pictures instead of a continuous development of an inherent pattern that moves according to its own nature.

Time, and life, is change. It is the nature of this change, or the way we perceive this change, that differs from East to West. We saw in the last chapter that change is a process which from its own essence creates a pattern and this pattern is the thread that runs through all life. By accepting the natural pattern we flow with life, rowing with the current, becoming the very stream that runs with us. By regarding every moment, in the Western tradition, as a separate picture, we turn every change into a crisis because each picture, each act, each movement along the way, is a turning point.

The second point follows from the first. The pattern of time itself is reflected in, and created by, the motion of the heavenly bodies. When we look at the Sun, the Moon and the planets moving through the sky, we perceive them as objective bodies acting upon another objective body. Thus the Sun moving through the ecliptic creates the Signs of the Zodiac. The Moon weaving its dance with the Sun and the earth creates the lunar phases. The earth turning upon its axis in relation to the ecliptic creates the diurnal Houses.

These three cycles, the zodiacal, the synodic (which produces the aspects and the phases), and the diurnal, are those generally used in astrology. Thus time is divided objectively into its seasons, into its generations and into its hours. But behind these cycles there exists the inherent cycles of the Sun, the Moon, the earth and the planets, and these create time itself. These make the pattern behind the pattern that we see. It is the web of life weaved by the gods like the web spun by a spider in space. This pattern is formed by the gods, or the heavenly bodies, from their own inherent nature because it is part of their inherent nature.

It is the nature of this inherent cycle, behind the cycles that are commonly used in astrology, that enables us to understand the underlying pattern of time. It is this cycle which provides the form of all the other cycles and which produces the changes and the crises that we see in the stream of time and of life. The inherent cycle of all the heavenly bodies is created by its motion. Motion, as we perceive it, is duality. In the East this duality is the yang and the yin, the continuous and the broken line. In the West we see duality in terms of opposites, positive and negative, black and white, odd and even.

As each of the bodies moves through its inherent cycle it changes its nature, and the nature of these changes, the crises as we see them, are always the same because they are part of the common pattern. At the mid-point of the cycle, yang changes to yin. At the mid-point of the yang and the yin a crisis is reached. And half-way between these four turning points a concentration of power is built up which evokes yet another form of crisis. Thus in every cycle eight main crisis points are produced and each of them is part of the natural order of change which develops in the march of time.

The inherent nature of change which is incorporated into the fabric of time is something that needs to be appreciated as the basis of electional astrology. For in elections we are doing two things. First, we are choosing the right moment for the success of an enterprise. This moment, symbolized in an electional horoscope, can be read on one level like any other horoscope. We can see the potentials, the conflicts and the problems of the enterpise by looking at the various factors and their relationships just as we can see these things in a birth or a mundane chart.

However, even here, there is a vital difference between elections and other branches of astrology. In electional astrology we are actively choosing a moment. If we understand the inherent dynamic of change that exists in the cycles of time we can ensure that the moment itself is at the right part of its cycle, for the cycles affect the nature of the moment. Second, we are also choosing an enterprise that will exist, and unfold, in the future. By appreciating the development of these inherent cycles we can ensure that the enterprise itself develops in the future according to the promise of the chosen time.

It is far from easy to see this underlying pattern because it involves a shift of perception from a view of the universe where objective things happen to one where there is a continuous stream which throws up from its own nature certain qualities. Nevertheless astrology is the science of time and without an understanding of the real nature of time astrology will fail to fulfill its potential. Moreover even astrologers tend to see time in the still moment rather than in the moving process of intrinsic change. I shall illustrate this change by looking at the solar cycle in the next section. In this way we shall see how the changes of the seasons turn from and into each other and how the nature of these changes provides the meaning for any particular time.

In looking at the way time changes in the last chapter, I concentrated on the simple pattern of interchanging forces that is used in the East. Western perception is more visual. Its culture is based on the symbolism of magic which incorporates the Kabbalah, the tarot and astrology in its tradition. The Signs of the Zodiac and the planets in astrology, the sephiroth and the paths in the Kabbalah and the major and minor arcana of the tarot are all perceived in visual images, pictures representing different aspects of life derived from archetypal principles that exist in the universe.

However, the underlying pattern is the same just as reality is the same however it is perceived. As the moment is not just a moment but part of the stream of time, so the pictures, the Signs, the sephiroth and the cards, are not just separate entities. Each is part of a pattern. By looking at the pattern in the simpler form of yang and yin in the last chapter we should be helped to see the same pattern behind the visual images of Western tradition, for behind the veil of manifestation all things are connected.

Magical philosophy, embracing the tenets of its derivatives including astrology, is based on the principle that the universe is a whole. Therefore the archetypal energies that exist in the universe are reflected in the heavens as they are on earth. God and man thus complement each other. Moreover the one God is divided in manifestation into certain specific forces. These forces, or principles, are symbolized by the sephiroth in the Kabbalah, by the planets in astrology and in their purer form as numbers in the tarot.

Each of these forces has its cycles in space and time and it is the function of magic to ensure that they are properly aligned for any particular enterprise. In astrology the forces are symbolized by the planets which correspond with the spatial and temporal aspects of manifestation on earth. In terms of space the quality of the universe is expressed through the senses in shape, colour, form, smell, movement and sound. In terms of time each planetary force has its tides and seasons.

In order to make the appropriate alignment it was therefore necessary first to decide on the intention, or the purpose, of the enterprise. Having decided on the intention, the corresponding planet would then rule the enterprise. If, for example, the intention was love, the relevant planet would be Venus. In temporal alignment Venus would be placed in the appropriate part of its cycle and in this way the various exaltations, rulerships, falls and detriments came into being. Moreover, the magician could go on to choose the day ruled by Venus, Friday, and the hour of that planet. We may recall from Chapter 2 how an image was made on Thursday during the hour of Jupiter from the metal of that planet.

In spatial alignment the correspondence in space according to the sensual quality of the intention would also be made. So, in accordance with the Venusian rite, the colour would be green, the metal copper, the scents ambergris, musk, myrtle or rose and so on. Astrology, as the time element of magic, deals only with time and it is this aspect of the universe alone which the astrologer aligns when he chooses the right time in elections.

But the pattern of time runs through the other systems I have mentioned, the Kabbalah and the tarot, for the same archetypal principles are symbolized in all these systems. In the Kabbalah the 10 sephiroth correspond with the Sun, the Moon, the earth and the seven planets. But the sephiroth are also numbers and by perceiving them as numbers we can see their natural development. For while numbers are on one level separate, they flow from each other. As one pours out and creates its successor, a pattern is created that itself creates the universe.

It is this outpouring that creates the same spatial and temporal pattern in the system of the tarot. Again, we can see two things in both the major and minor arcana. For each card is at once a pictorial image and also a number. In the minor arcana each suit runs from the 1 to the 10. And the progression in the numbers can be seen in its natural development through the numbers according to the nature of each suit. Thus, in the beginning, at the 1 or Ace, is the seed, the potential or power for the quality represented in that suit.

As the 1 splits into the 2, so the Tao divides into the yang and the yin and there is opposition, dilemma and conflict. This conflict is then resolved in the 3 when a new force is produced from the polarity of the 2. Here there is reconciliation which forms into a tangible and material structure in the 4. To get beyond this point, the structure must be broken down. Here, at the 5, the mid-point of the sequence, is the greatest crisis, and in their own way all the fives represent conflict and difficulty. And so the pattern unfolds until the 10 is reached which shows how the quality of the suit must be dealt with.

The pattern of time also runs through and creates the thread of the major arcana. These cards represented to the medieval minds (who in all probability were the first to use them) the archetypal story of existence. So, on one level, they portray the road of the hero as he or she steps out on life's journey, the choices and the challenges that are made and met by everyman, in relationships, in ambition, in sickness, in spiritual isolation.

On another level the circle runs its course. The main crisis points are indeed different ways of perceiving the circles that represent time and eternity, bondage and freedom. In the first, the circle of the number 0 where the Fool sets off on his journey, there is freedom, but a freedom born of innocence and ignorance. Half-way through the cycle, in the number 10, we meet the second circle, the Wheel of Fortune. Here, as at the mid-point of our own lives symbolized in astrology by the Uranus opposition, we are turned upside down as we are forced to face the past before we can progress into the future.

This is the central card in the sequence, the Whitsun zenith where the gods stay in mid-heaven, but where Man is thrown down, cling though he may to the past. Here he is circumscribed, chained to the circle of life's never-ending cycles. When he learns the meaning of these cycles he can rise again and at the last card, in the final circle, the Universe, he can dance free, returning in his wisdom to the liberty of his first foolish step into the world.

Combining the separate visual images in the Western systems, whether they be the Signs of the Zodiac or the cards in the tarot, with the underlying pattern that runs through these images, enables us to see beneath the surface of life and view the thread of time. Although the perception is different in East and West, the reality is the same. Through Eastern eyes we saw the interplay of yang and yin forces creating change. We saw how, at the extreme point of each force, it turned into its opposite.

Through Western eyes we have seen how time develops and how at the top the wheel is reversed whereas at the bottom the tide rises again until once more it turns. These changes, the crises that form the turning points of life, are inherent in every cycle. They can be seen in mundane phenomena such as the rise and fall of the stock market as they can be seen in life itself. Their understanding is vital in the study of elections both in choosing the time itself, for these changes are inherent in time and affect its nature, and in choosing the future of the enterprise, for the future changes in time according to its inherent pattern.

Some people, with their instinctive sense of timing that comes from an intuitive perception of the universe, are aware of these inherent changes that, in crisis, throw up their opposites. George Eliot, for example, came to recognize the signs of her impending illness because just before the occurrence of ill-health she would feel, in her words, 'dangerously well'. We can see in the following examples how the wheel turned at two important crisis points in the lives of famous men.

When Verdi reached the age of 29, at the time of his first Saturn Return, his life was in ruins. His first child, Virginia, had died the year before when only 17 months old. Then his second, and only remaining child, Icilio Romano, died just 16 months of age. Verdi himself was confined to bed with a bad attack of angina for several weeks. When he got better his wife, Margherita, died. A friend said that at this time Verdi was 'on the point of mental aberration'. In this state of severe depression he completed his opera *Un Giorn di Regno*. It was to be his worst failure. Verdi never forgot the humiliation, the laughter and the catcalls, which forced the opera to be withdrawn after its first performance.

In a mood of black despair he gave up his house in Milan and took a furnished room in the Piazzeta San Romano. He saw no one, became apathetic and hardly left the building. He wrote: 'I persuaded myself that I had nothing more to find in music and I decided never to compose again.'[1] Then at the nadir of his life, as he suffered the crucifixion of Saturn, he met Bartolomeo Merelli, the powerful manager of Milan's La Scala who showed him a libretto. That meeting was the beginning of *Nabucco* and it was the turning point of Verdi's creative life. On the morning of *Nabucco's* première on 9 March 1842 Verdi literally woke up and found himself famous.

At the other extreme, the year 1895 marked the height of Oscar Wilde's success. Then at the age of 40, when Uranus opposed its natal position, he found himself at the pinnacle of fame and fortune. *An Ideal Husband* had its première at the Haymarket on 3 January, while *The Importance of Being Earnest* played to a tumultuous audience at the St James on its first night on 14 February. Wilde wrote to Ada Leverson: 'The gods had given me almost everything. I had genius, a distinguished name, high social position, brilliancy, intellectual daring: I made art a philosophy and philosophy an art; I altered the minds of men and the colours of things; there was nothing I said or did that did not make people wonder.'[2]

But then at the zenith the gods revoked their gifts. And the momentum of change was devastating in its abruptness as Wilde in his sublime blindness disregarded the symptoms of his dangerous well-being. At the end of February he applied for a warrant charging the Marquess of Queensberry with criminal libel. On 5 April Wilde himself was arrested and by the end of May he had been sentenced to the maximum term of two years' imprisonment with hard labour. The wheel had come full circle.

The seasons in the West and the ritual year

The nature of the inherent cycle of all the heavenly bodies can most readily be exemplified by the annual seasons, the cycle created by the Sun as it travels along the ecliptic. We discussed the principle of the cycle in the last section. Now we shall see how it works out in practice during the course of the year.

I have chosen the Sun's cycle because it is the one we are most familiar with. Everyone is aware of the seasons, of the changes that occur throughout the year as the Sun gains and loses its power. The Sun's path also creates the Signs of the Zodiac which are known to the majority of people. But the underlying pattern of this cycle, with

its points of crisis and change, is one that exists in the cycles of the
Moon, the planets, the earth itself. We shall therefore be looking
not only at the events thrown up along the Sun's way but also at
the common thread that creates the same changes and the same crises
as each heavenly body develops its own inherent cycle.

The ancients were even more aware of the Sun's power and its effects
upon their lives. Although there is evidence of a previous Moon
worship upon which the calendar was based, by neolithic times society
had integrated a Sun-oriented fertility cult which lingered into the
Iron Age, producing solar temples throughout the world, from the
Red Indian culture to Stonehenge and the temples of Babylon.

In this country, for example, we find Diodorus Siculus reporting
in 350 BC that Hecateus of Abdera had written: 'Opposite to the
land of the Celts there exists in the ocean an island no smaller than
Sicily. The inhabitants honour Apollo more than any other. A sacred
enclosure is dedicated to him in the island, as well as a magnificent
circular temple adorned with many offerings.'[3]

That the neolithic Sun-god should become first the prime source
of the cult of Mythras and then the Son of God in the Christian
religion should cause no surprise. As St John Chrysostom stated in
De solstitiis et aequinoctiis: 'But the Lord too, was born in wintertime,
on the 25th of December, when the ripe olives are pressed in order
to produce the oil for anointing, the chrism. They also call this day
the birthday of the "Unconquerable One". Yet who is as
unconquerable as our Lord, who overthrew and conquered death
itself? He himself is the Sun of righteousness of whom the prophet
Malachi spoke. He is the Lord of light and darkness.'[4]

By being aware of the times created by the path of the Sun the
ancients produced and performed their rites and rituals, their religious
festivals and liturgy, at the appropriate times. However, it was not
the Sun alone that was worshipped. The old festivals took place also
under the watchful eye of the Moon as the great female power of
the universe. Moreover the worship of the Sun itself was in reality
a sacred drama acted out between the Sun and the earth, the god
and the goddess who played through their intimate relationship
during the course of each year.

It is the Sun's relationship with the earth that creates the Zodiac.
And it is the relationship between the yang or solar power and the
yin or earth force that produces the dynamic of change and the
seasons. We can now trace the pattern of the seasons as they are played
out by the god and the goddess, bearing in mind the more abstract
symbolism of the yang and the yin that we described in the last

chapter. In Fig. 5.1 we can see the general pattern in time which exists in the year, the month and the day and which produces the same points of crisis in each cycle.

The Sun's cycle begins in the Sign of its exaltation, Aries, when the strength of the god is most potent. Conversely, the solar energy has waned by the time it has reached Libra, the Sign of its fall when the goddess becomes dominant. Thus the first division of the year is into two, the first half, from the vernal equinox, being yang, while the second, from the autumn equinox, being yin.

The yang half of the year is the time for pursuing active endeavours, for assertiveness and breaking new ground. The beginning of the solar year especially symbolizes the beginning of an enterprise as new life thrusts through the barren earth. The yin half, on the contrary, when the earth is replenished and stores up the potential of the future within its womb, is appropriate for receptive endeavours.

The yang and yin halves of the year are themselves further divided into two, creating the four seasons. The predominantly active time of spring gives way to the plenitude of summer, while the nurturing of autumn is withdrawn into the darkening of winter. Finally each season is divided into three phases, a beginning, a middle and an end, which correspond with the Cardinal, Fixed and Mutable Modes producing the 12 Signs of the Zodiac.

The point of entry into the seasons, and the mid-points of the seasons, are times of great potency. They are times of change on the one hand and concentration of power on the other. The major alterations in the pattern of energy occur at the beginning of the four seasons when each of the four Elements is introduced. In its most simplified form we can see how these changes operate by returning to the Eastern view of the interplay between yang and yin. At the times of the equinoxes the yang and the yin are equal. Here we have balance, yet this balance is only momentary. In the very moment of achievement it is destroyed, for in reality the motion never stops.

So at the equinoxes the most profound changes of alignment take place. As the universe is a whole these changes can be seen at every level, as the equinoctial winds blow harshly, overturning the delicate balance of the forces of nature. We usually regard the vernal equinox as the beginning of the year as Aries is the first Sign of the Zodiac. This indeed is the time when new life is born, when the young shoots push through the stubborn soil of winter and the earth is renewed. But both equinoxes are beginnings; the autumn equinox is the beginning of the yin half of the year when the fruit falls to rejuvenate the earth for the coming spring.

The beginning and the end are thus the same as the cycles run full circle. Each beginning is an end and each end a beginning. In terms of choosing the right time what matters, as always, is the specific kind of enterprise with which we are concerned. If the enterprise is of a yang nature, active, opportunist, then the yang half of the year, and especially the vernal equinox which signifies beginnings in general, will be the right time. If, on the other hand, we are concerned with yin matters, then the yin half of the year, and in particular the autumn equinox which reflects the onset of fruitful completion, will be the appropriate time.

At the solstices, when the Sun enters the remaining seasons, summer and winter, we have change of a different kind. Here, at this still point in time, each force, the yang and the yin, is at its most potent. At the summer solstice the yang power has reached its highest point but, as we have seen in the last chapter, the existence of one force alone is an illusion, for the yang itself consists of the yin, if only in potential.

The importance of the solstices lies in the fact that when any force reaches its maximum state it turns into its opposite. When the top is attained, the only way on is down; when the bottom is encountered, we can only rise again. This of course was the message of the Wheel of Fortune which we saw played out in different ways in the lives of Verdi and Wilde. And it is as true in all spheres of life, in the stock market as in the future of marriages and governments.

So the summer solstice represents the height of the yang force: plentitude, the fullness of life. The winter solstice, on the other hand, reflects the greatest strength of the receptive energy, the yin, the seed being nurtured in the womb of the earth goddess, leading to the emergence and promise of new life germinating in the darkness, and the eventual triumph of the light.

The equinoxes and the solstices are the quarter days. The mid-points of these four times, which thus fall in the middle of the Fixed Signs, are the cross-quarter-days. Here too we have change and crisis but of a different kind. While the beginning of the seasons marks the entry of a new kind of energy into the universe, symbolized by the Sun moving into the Cardinal Signs of the four Elements, the cross-quarter days are those when the energies are at their most concentrated. Then the Sun has reached the middle of the Fixed Signs of those four Elements. Here there is a build-up of power which can be explosive if not contained and channelled.

These eight points in the year mark the great periods of power and each is marked by one of the great religious festivals. The importance of the cross-quarter days was especially recognized by the Celts who divided their year into four parts, each being introduced by a festival which commemorated a cult legend. Owing to the change in the calendar the dates of these festivals have shifted and they are now at the end of October, January, April and July as can be seen in Fig. 5.1.

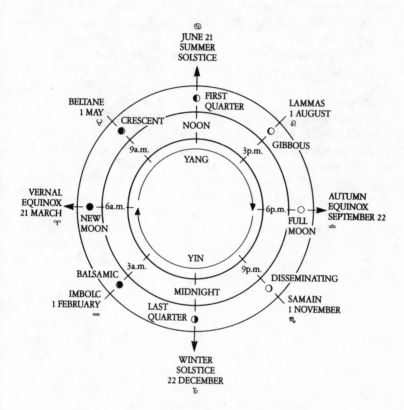

Figure 5.1 The cycles of the Sun, Moon and Earth

In fact the actual moment of power is at midnight on the last day of the month when the current of power crosses over. Thus the preceding day has a negative connotation and atmosphere, and is generally regarded as evil, while the following day, the first of the month, is positive. This can now be seen in the Christian version of the festivals. Because the power is so intense during these periods, and because the currents cross, these times, as well as the quarter-

days, are times when the gates between our world and other planes
are open, when the ghosts, gods and departed spirits are free to move
upon the earth.

The Celtic year began on the night preceding the feast of Samain,
1 November. It was on this night of Hallowe'en in particular that
the otherworld became visible to mankind and the forces of the
supernatural world were let loose upon the human plane. As always,
the beginning and the end were the same for it was then that the
Sun god, or hero, having played out his sacred drama with the earth
goddess, was slain.

The next cross-quarter day, 1 February, was Imbolc or Oimelg,
sacred to the goddess Brigit, who was subsequently Christianized
as St Brigid, and according to the agrarian pattern of the year was
connected with the coming into milk of the ewes. Beltane was on
1 May and the promotion of fertility can still be seen in the symbolism
of the Maypole. Like many of the Celtic festivals the solar power
symbolized by fire was apparent. At this time bonfires were kindled
and the cattle were driven through the flames in order to purify them.

The period of the Sun god extended only from May Day or the
summer solstice and ended, once more at his height, at the time
of the First Fruits Feast on the next cross-quarter-day, 1 August,
although the final death and promise of regeneration occurred at
the following cross-quarter day in Scorpio, at Hallowe'en. So, far from
being omnipotent, the reign of the solar Hero was comparatively
short. Moreover, it was his function to impregnate the earth goddess,
who was immortal, and this task performed, he was doomed to die
at the close of summer.

The sacred drama was played out in the form of the corn idol,
or dolly, sometimes called John Barleycorn, which was ritually killed
and buried during the ploughing that followed the harvest so that
the cycle of birth, death and rebirth could be repeated. It was indeed
at the time of the harvest that the Celtic year was centred, naturally
enough for an early pastoral community.

The central point was Lammas, the cross-quarter-day on 1 August,
the mid-point of Leo, the Sign of the Sun's rulership. This was the
great agrarian feast sometimes called Lughnasa after the god of light,
Lugos or Lugh. Although the summer solstice, or midsummer, is
the beginning of summer and the longest day, it is at the beginning
of August that the Sun is at its most powerful, and generally the
hottest time of the year in our Northern latitudes. The festival itself
lasted for a month, starting 15 days before Lammas and continuing
for a further 15 after that date, and then the Sun began his slow

climb down until the final death of the god on 31 October, the end, and the beginning, of the annual cycle.

Having looked at the general pattern of the solar cycle I want now to look in more detail at the year so that we can recognize the qualities of the times and become aware of the inner meaning of this cycle. As we do so we shall see that the year is centred on the eight points I have just highlighted, not as isolated periods but as parts of a continuum. I shall illustrate these points of crisis and change in the year by looking at some important events, first in history generally, and second, during one particular year, that of 1985 when this book was being prepared.

As we follow the Sun's path in this way we shall see the pattern emerging. We shall see how the quality of any particular time, which was recognized in Christian and in pagan myth, is mirrored in events and we shall also see how the events rise to a climax around the actual quarter or cross-quarter days and then, once the crisis is past, level out again until they build up towards the next time of change or concentration of power. So the pattern continually repeats itself, rising and falling and rising again.

We can conveniently start the year at the time of the winter solstice or Christmas. As we have seen, at this time the yin force is at its most potent. In the extreme darkness of the winter the light is extinguished. The Sun, the yang force, has died, but in dying it needs to be born again. Although we cannot see the shoots beneath the barren ground or the Sun's rays before the dawn, they are about to appear.

So in pagan times the Yule-log was lit for Thor to represent warmth and the continuance of the light. The Emperor Aurelian celebrated the festival *Natalis Invicti Solis* (Birth of the Unconquerable Sun), in AD 274, as part of the cult of Mithras. So when Christianity superseded the old religions midnight mass was celebrated to welcome the appearance of the light in the depths of darkness. And at dawn on Christmas Day, the birthday of the Son of God, the Aurora mass celebrates the rising Sun which illuminates and transfigures the world, opening with the introit *Lux fulgebit* (A light shall shine upon us this day, for our Lord is born to us).

The beginning of winter is the low point of the year, the time of darkness for the spirit as well as the days. When the yang forces are depleted there is a negative quality which is reflected in physical ill-health and in mental despondency and depression as can be seen in the rates of suicides and road accidents. But, as in all cases, the lowest point occurs around the following cross-quarter day, 1 February, which is also the coldest time of the year.

This is when the negative forces are most concentrated for they have built up to crisis point and people's energies are at their lowest ebb. But the opposites are contained in each other and, just as at the winter solstice the Sun is born, so at this darkest hour the goddess of nature returns in the form of Diana. In Rome the goddess Februata Juno represented mating, and the fertility of flocks, herds and women. Her feast of *Lupercalia*, held on 15 February, owing to the displacement of the calendar became associated with St Valentine's Day on 14 February (also known as Old Candlemas). In Egypt the Festival of Lights was associated with the goddess Isis.

Christianity, as was its wont, took over the dedication of light as Candlemas when all the lights which are to be used in the ceremonies during the year are blessed. And in place of Isis, the Christian Church substituted the Virgin Mary, 1 February now being the Feast of the Purification of the Blessed Virgin Mary when the infant Christ was presented in the temple as, in the words of Simeon in the Nunc Dimittis: 'the light to lighten the Gentiles, and to be the glory of thy people Israel.'

When we look at events in the world we can see the moment coming to its crisis with a pattern of gradually worsening situations, reaching their peak on the cross-quarter day after which things level off. On 21 January, Louis XVI was guillotined and Lenin died. On the following day Queen Victoria died. General Gordon was killed at Khartoum on the 26th and in 1939 Barcelona fell to the Spanish Nationalists. In 1985 a detective constable from Scotland Yard was stabbed to death when he tried to serve a search warrant at a house in Kent. Reflecting the former event, on the 28th, just two days later, an assistant in a London shoe shop was stabbed to death by a customer who said his shoes were unsatisfactory. Two apparently motiveless, unprovoked deaths by stabbing as the cross-quarter day approaches.

Also on the 28th, Paris surrendered to the German army in 1871 and Henry VIII died. On the 30th Crown Prince Rudolf of Austria and Mary Vetsera committed suicide at Mayerling; Mahatma Ghandi was assassinated, Charles I was executed and Adolt Hitler was appointed Chancellor of Germany. On the following day Guy Fawkes was hanged and Trotsky expelled from Russia. On a smaller scale Crippen murdered his wife in 1910. On 1 February itself King Carlos I of Portugal was assassinated in 1908 and in 1917 Germany began unrestricted warfare.

From now on we can see the pattern gradually improving both in the absence of events like the above and also by more positive ones. On 2 February the Germans capitulated at Stalingrad in 1943, while in 1985, on the 4th, Desmond Tutu was enthroned as the first black Anglican bishop of Johannesburg. In 1985, on the 5th, Spain opened its border gates with Gibraltar for the first time since 1969 and four Britons held in Libya for almost nine months were released.

After winter comes the spring. The seed planted at the winter solstice breaks through the earth and the solar year begins. But the time of birth is the time of death when Christ, born in the dead of winter, dies to the world at the equinox. In pagan myth, in the sacred drama of the god and goddess, the Sun mates to produce a new Sun born at the winter solstice in nine months' time.

The theme of death and rebirth is one that runs through the various religions at this point. Odin sacrificed himself by hanging on Yggdrasil, the World Tree, for nine nights. Attis fell in love with Cybele, the goddess of flowers and fruitfulness. He was gored by a wild boar and bled to death, in an act of self-sacrifice, under a pine tree. The day of his death, 22 March, was celebrated as a day of blood and fasting, followed three days later, on the 25th, by the Hilaria, a day of rejoicing for his resurrection.

Similarly the body of Osiris was found in a giant tamarisk tree, while Christ was hanged on a tree three days before his resurrection at the feast of Easter, named after the Saxon deity Eostre, the goddess of the dawn. And at midnight on Easter Day, the New Fire is blessed and the Paschal Taper is lit which then burns through the 40 days until Ascension, representing the period Christ spent on earth after his resurrection.

Turning to world events, the negative pattern once more builds up towards the equinox when the tide turns specifically to new beginnings. On 18 March King George of Greece was assassinated in 1913, while in 1848 the Italian Revolution broke out in Milan. On the 21st Archbishop Cranmer was burnt at the stake, the Duc d'Enghien was shot leading to a universal outcry and condemnation of Napoleon, and the battle of the Somme began in 1918. In 1985 on that day the South African police opened fire on a crowd of 4000 blacks on their way to a funeral, killing 19 and injuring more than 30, and in the Lebanon, Israeli troops raided villages killing more than 20 suspected terrorists.

At the equinox the tide turns, and, to reflect the beginning of the solar year on the 23rd, Pakistan was proclaimed an Islamic Republic in 1956, while the Greeks announced their independence in 1821 on the 25th, and became a republic on the same day in 1924. Also on that day the Treaty of Rome established the EEC in 1957.

The following cross-quarter day, 1 May, lies at the centre of the

fertility cult at the high climactic point of spring. So May Eve is the
pagan wedding of the god and goddess, when the Hunter, as the
god, chases his mate, the White Hind. Beltane, or May Day,
represents the return of summer and the battle between the May
Queen and the Queen of Winter. The power of this day was
recognized as St Walburga's Day, the great witches' festival, which
Christianity attempted to take over as the Feast of the Apparition
of St Michael, symbolizing victory over the Devil – with singular
lack of success.

The resolute catalogue of negative events presages this time too.
On 25 April the guillotine was first erected in Paris in 1792. On the
26th Guernica was destroyed by the Germans in 1937. On the 28th
Mussolini was executed in 1945, while the mutiny on the 'Bounty'
took place in 1789 and in 1969 General de Gaulle resigned as
President of France. On the 30th Adolf Hitler committed suicide
and in 1926 the General Strike began in Britain.

Summer comes with the solstice around 21 June and Midsummer's
Day is the 24th. This point in the year, opposing the winter solstice,
makes an equally interesting paradox. For just as birth comes in the
depth of winter, so death threatens at the height of summer.
Midsummer Eve is traditionally known as the night when fairies are
abroad. Amusing though this idea may appear, it has long been
accepted that at midnight between Midsummer Eve and Day the
gates between heaven and earth are open.

To this day, a sect called the Circle sets out from the church of
St John the Baptist in Glastonbury and makes it ways to the Tor where
the remains of St Michael's church stand in memory of that saint's
embodiment of the solar power. For it is at this time that the angels
guarding the earth are reported to change and hence the earth stands
in danger of invasion from the forces of evil. St John the Baptist has
indeed been identified with the ancient fire festival that took place
on this day which is now his feast day. Nor is it any coincidence that
the herald and baptizer of Christ should have his festival at the exact
opposition to the birth of his Lord.

In world events we find the Emperor Maximilian of Mexico shot
on 19 June 1867. On the 20th Louis XVI was captured when he tried
to escape to Varennes in 1791, while on the same day in 1792 the
mob invaded the Tuileries. On the 21st in 1919 the German fleet
was scuttled in Scapa Flow, while on the same day in 1942 Tobruk
fell to the Germans. On the 22nd Bishop John Fisher was executed
in 1535 and on the 23rd in 1793 the Reign of Terror began in France.
On the 25th we find the execution of Earl Rivers and Earl Grey by

Richard III in 1483, General Custer's last stand at the battle of Little Big Horn in 1876 and the beginning of the Korean War in 1950.

In 1985 a series of explosions occurred in different parts of the world. On the 18th an RUC officer was killed when a landmine exploded under his car. The pace quickened on the 19th when three people, including two children, were killed by bomb explosions in the departure lounge of Frankfurt airport. Then on the 23rd, 329 passengers were killed when an Air India Boeing 747 crashed into the Atlantic, apparently caused by a bomb explosion. On the same day two freight handlers were killed in Nasita airport in Japan when a bomb exploded in a container, and finally a bomb was discovered and defused in the Rubens hotel near Buckingham Palace in London.

Summer reaches its sultry heights on the cross-quarter-day of Lammas, a word meaning 'loaf mass' when the last sheaf of corn was made into the form of Cernunnos, the antlered solar god, and the god was cut down and laid in the arms of the goddess. In Egypt the day was sacred to Isis and of vital importance as the beginning of the inundation of the Nile when new life was brought back to the land. Just as the opposite cross-quarter-day on 2 February was dedicated by Christianity to its female version of the deity in the form of the Virgin Mary, so originally 2 August, and subsequently the 15th, became the Feast of the Assumption.

On the world stage a revolution began in Paris on 27 July 1830, while on the 29th the Spanish Armada was routed in 1588 and on the 31st the third battle of Ypres began in 1917. On 1 August the Central Powers declared war on Russia in 1914 and in 1934 on that date Hitler became Reichsfuhrer. On 2 August 1914, Germany declared war on France.

We have seen that the autumn equinox is as much a time of new beginnings in its own way as it is of fulfilment, when former ideas are brought to material realization and past efforts are rewarded. So on the 21st we see the beginning of the French Republic in 1792, while in 1949 the Federal Republic of Germany formally came into existence and the People's Republic of China was proclaimed on the same day. On the 25th the battle of Stamford Bridge in 1066 effectively heralded Harold's defeat by William the Conqueror who was crowned at precisely the next quarter day, 25 December.

Hallowe'en's baleful influence marks the most intensely negative time in the Sign of Scorpio when the atmosphere of death can be felt by anyone with even a little sensitivity. Christianity's acceptance of this reality is apparent in its naming 1 November All Saints' Day and the 2nd, All Souls'.

Leading up to this time we find Sir Walter Raleigh executed on 29 October 1618, the German Mutiny beginning exactly 300 years later at the end of the First World War and then the Suez Canal debacle and the Hungarian uprising occurring simultaneously in international counterpoint. The attack on the canal began on the 29th, while the air offensive of Egypt set out on the very night of Hallowe'en. The parallel Hungarian uprising which had begun on 23 October was crushed when the Russians returned with reinforcements on Hallowe'een.

Also on Hallowe'en we find Martin Luther, appropriately with his Sun in Scorpio, nailing his theses on indulgences to the church door at Wittenberg in 1517, and another person with Sun in Scorpio, Indira Gandhi, being assassinated on the same day in 1984. Scorpio's association with earthquakes and revolutions can also be seen immediately after Hallowe'en. On 1 November, the great earthquake erupted at Lisbon in 1755, almost destroying the city. On the 3rd, Abruzzi was destroyed in 1706. On the 4th the German Revolution broke out in 1918, while the October Revolution took place in Russia on the 7th in 1917.

The lunar, planetary and diurnal cycles

Each heavenly body has its inherent cycle. Each inherent cycle has the qualities that we have seen exemplified in the cycle of the Sun. Each has a yang half followed by a yin half; each has the four points of change which begins its seasons; and finally each has the cross-quarter points where the greatest power is concentrated, producing in all the eight crisis points that we have noted.

As the heavenly bodies pass through their different cycles, the zodiacal, the synodic and the diurnal, it is easy to lose sight of the inherent cycle. Indeed in many cases the cycles coincide. The inherent cycle of the Sun, for example, is also the zodiacal cycle because the Sun creates the Zodiac. Nevertheless the nature of the cycles is different. The zodiacal cycle is descriptive and each body describes a particular quality of time as it proceeds through the Signs.

Therefore it is the nature of the cycle itself that is important. The quality, though not the quantity, of time is the same in all the inherent cycles. And this quality lies behind the surface of the other cycles. When I looked at the solar cycle in the last section I did not mention the Signs themselves because I was concerned with the thread that formed the underlying pattern. In the same way, when we are concerned with the underlying structure of time, the time that dwells beneath the surface, we need to concentrate on the unfolding of the inherent cycle of each heavenly body.

Thus each inherent cycle is concerned with beginnings, fulfilment, completion and promise and with the crises and changes that are indrawn into the phases of time. The yang half is the time for active involvement while the yin half is for receptive concentration. And this pattern is repeated in the year with the Sun's cycle, in the month with the lunar cycle, in the day with the earth's cycle and in the varying periods of time, from generation to generation, in the planetary cycles.

If we look once more at Fig. 5.1, we can see how the cycles of the Sun, Moon and earth coincide. The inherent cycles of the planets also coincide as they travel from exaltation to exaltation but with their different periods it is not practicable to superimpose them in the same way. Furthermore, the practice of elections depends on selecting the factors in an order of relative importance, and the inherent cycles of the planets is of far less importance than their zodiacal cycles.

The inherent lunar cycle coincides with its phases. Just as the Sun's cycle forms the relationship between the Sun and the earth whereby the male power of the solar hero fertilizes the earth mother to provide a new cycle of life, so the Moon's phases form the relationship between the light of the Sun god and the Moon goddess, whereby the sacred drama of life and death is played out.

So the phase from New to Full Moon is yang, reflecting the vernal to the autumn equinox in the solar cycle. This phase in general, when the Moon is waxing, is the time for new beginnings, for outgoing enterprises, for building up. Conversely, the phase from Full to New Moon, or the waning period, coincides with the autumn to the vernal equinox. This is the time for reaping rather than sowing, for cutting down rather than planting, for receiving rather than giving.

In the same way, the Quarter Moons coincide with the solstices and are times of plenitude and promise, periods of potency and withdrawal when changes take place. Equally, the mid-points of these four times are periods when the power of the lunar force is concentrated. We shall see the way these times reflect the hard aspects when we look at them in more detail in the second half of the book.

The same pattern is present in the earth's inherent cycle as it turns on its axis from dawn to noon, to dusk, to midnight, before a new dawn breaks once more. So the period from dawn to dusk is the yang phase while that from dusk to dawn is the yin. Dawn, the time of freshness and awakening, has the same quality as spring. Noon is the time of satiety, heaviness and plenitude, with the Sun reaching its zenith as it does at midsummer. Dusk is a time of quiet, calm and reflection coinciding with the gradual peace of autumn's fall. Midnight, the witching hour when the earth is still, is reminiscent of the winter solstice.

The cross-quarter days of the year coincide too with the crisis times of the day; 3 a.m. and 3 p.m. and, to a lesser extent, 9 a.m. and 9 p.m. are the times of the day when the energies are especially potent just as the other four times, reflecting the solar seasons, are times of change. These are 6 a.m., noon, 6 p.m. and midnight. If we look at the pattern of illness, for example, as a reflection of the physical currents during its daily pattern, we can see these times of crisis and change at work; 3 a.m. and 3 p.m., in particular, are times of birth and death, when the body is at its lowest ebb, while disease will frequently reach its turning point at 6 p.m. and midnight and once more at 6 a.m. and noon.

In times gone by, when the spirit of religion reflected the pattern of time and the world of manifestation more nearly, these periods were beautifully symbolized by the archangels who protected, and still protect, the earth. Raphael rises with the Sun in the East while Michael stands, sword drawn, guardian at the midday zenith; Gabriel blesses as the Sun sinks over the horizon, and Uriel keeps the midnight hour. Even today, 3 o'clock in the morning, the lowest point in the diurnal cycle, is known as the canonical hour of the crucifixion. The truth of course remains, and will remain, beneath the symbols whichever gods reign.

6.

ALL PAST YEARS: THE PRACTICAL ASPECTS OF TIME

I am going to end the first half of this book by looking at the horoscopes of some well-known events. In this way we shall see how the differing qualities of time are reflected both by the heavenly bodies which are the symbols of astrology and by the situations that occur in time. The events I have chosen are mainly those of major national and international catastrophes. Not only do these illustrate times which are of great significance in themselves but they also show what should be avoided in selecting a time, something which in practice is as important as knowing which factors should be chosen.

For the most part, too, I have chosen two horoscopes which reflect the same kind of event. The aim is not of course to provide statistical evidence for any particular occurrence but simply to illustrate the points made in this book so far. So we can see how, from the descriptive viewpoint, the quality of time is reflected in the positions of the Sun, Moon and planets, how the greater cycles of the planets are reflected in the moment by the Angles as crises occur, and how specific problems are brought into manifestation through the diurnal cycle.

The first pair of horoscopes I have chosen are connected with nuclear explosions. The first (see Fig. 6.1) is for the time the atom bomb was dropped on Hiroshima at 8.16 a.m. on 6 August 1945. The second (see Fig. 6.2) is that of the Chernobyl nuclear disaster on 26 April 1986, mirrored on that day by prison riots in this country which ended in Northeye prison at Bexhill-on-Sea being burnt to the ground. If we look at the second horoscope first, we get a good view of time as a continuum. The Sun is closely opposed to Pluto from Taurus to Scorpio. The Moon's position would not be regarded as critical in this particular example as the only hard aspect it makes is an opposition to Venus, but in terms of continuity it is in Scorpio and, having passed over Pluto, is moving towards Saturn and approaching Uranus, Neptune and Mars.

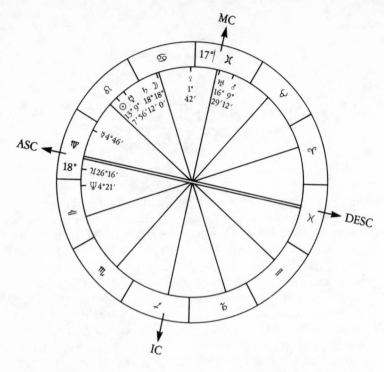

Figure 6.1 Horoscope for the bombing of Hiroshima
8.16 a.m. LT, 6 August 1945, Hiroshima (34N23, 132E30)

Mercury's position is of interest. As the ruler of communication, it would govern a power plant. In practice problems frequently occur when difficult aspects are made to this body which acts as a general communicator of events. Here we find it in Aries squaring both Mars and Neptune, which symbolizes the nuclear explosion and subsequent radiation that covered large expanses of the earth. Finally, to coincide with the explosion almost to the minute, we have Uranus within a degree of the Sagittarian Ascendant at 22 degrees 50 minutes.

Turning to the horoscope for Hiroshima, we find Uranus once more close to an Angle, this time at 16 degrees 29 minutes of Gemini with the Midheaven at 16 degrees 47 minutes. Here too the Sun and Pluto are in hard aspect and Mercury is again square Mars. The Moon's position is of even greater interest, applying to an almost exact conjunction with Saturn, only 12 minutes of arc apart, in Cancer. The Moon in Cancer conjunct Saturn is incidentally to be found

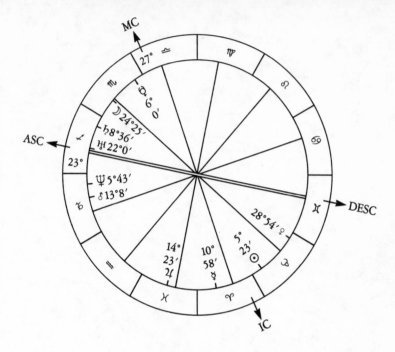

Figure 6.2 Horoscope for the Chernobyl disaster
1.23 a.m. LT, 26 April 1986, Chernobyl, USSR (51N17, 30E15)

in the birth charts of two recent mass murderers, Dennis Nilsen who holds the current record for murder in this country, and Peter Sutcliffe, the 'Yorkshire Ripper'.

We may also note the other side of this horoscope. From the point of view of the victims, the men, women and children who watched a single plane drop its bomb from a clear, blue summer sky on the morning of the Transfiguration, that moment was the beginning of a horrifying nightmare. To those who have watched with despair as nuclear weapons proliferate and threaten the peoples of the world, that nightmare is continuing. Yet Jupiter rises in this chart and squares Venus, and Neptune too is part of the complex. The rationale for Hiroshima was the hope that the war with Japan would be ended and that result was certainly achieved. Hope, however misconceived, and the means to provide its promise, is written into this chart.

The next pair are the Munich air crash of 1958 when 21 people, including seven of the Manchester United football team, were killed

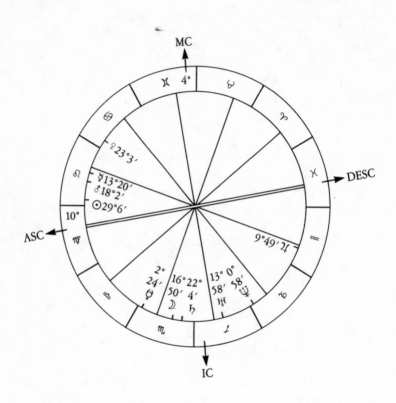

Figure 6.3 Horoscope for the Manchester Airport crash
7.13 a.m. BST, 22 August 1985, Manchester (53N30, 2W15)

when their BEA Elizabethan airliner crashed in a heavy snowstorm,
and the Manchester Airport crash in August 1985 when 54 people
died after their jet exploded on the runway. Again, taking the latter
horoscope first (see Fig. 6.3), we can see Mercury, ruling journeys,
conjunct Mars in the Fire Sign of Leo in the 12th House and making
a T-square with Jupiter and the Moon.

The Moon once again is applying to a conjunction with Saturn,
this time in Scorpio. In the Munich air crash (see Fig. 6.4) there is

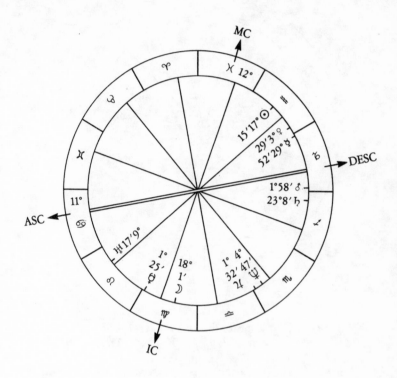

Figure 6.4 Horoscope for the Munich air crash
2.04 p.m. LT, 6 February 1958, Munich, Germany (48N08, 11E34)

another T-square involving Mercury, which is conjunct Venus, square Jupiter and Neptune and opposite to Uranus. Here too we find the Moon applying to a hard aspect with Saturn, coming up to a square from its position in Virgo.

Next we can look at two fires on the ground, both in Yorkshire. On 9 July 1984 a bolt of lightning started a fire which threatened to destroy York Minster. The south transept was burnt and extensively damaged but fortunately no one was injured and the rest of the

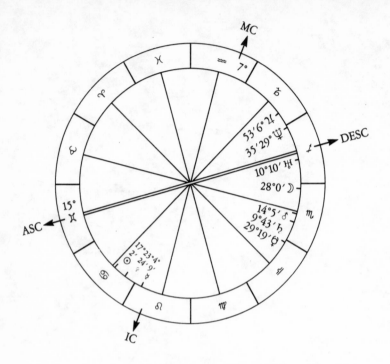

Figure 6.5 Horoscope for the York Minster fire
2.32 a.m. BST, 9 July 1984, York (53N58, 1W05)

building was saved. Now, after four years of careful work, the Minster
has been restored. The horoscope for this event (see Fig. 6.5) is a
far less difficult one than those of other disasters I have selected and
in particular the Moon makes no hard aspects. Mercury is close to
the IC and squares both Saturn and Pluto, the aspect falling near
to the mid-point of those planets, and Pluto was stationary on that
day. Uranus was also approaching the Descendant when the lightning
struck. Mars too is conjunct Saturn in Scorpio on the cusp of the
6th House.

We can contrast this horoscope with that of the Bradford football
stadium fire when over 50 people were burned to death and many
others were seriously injured in one of the most horrific incidents
in this country. To reflect the general situation at that time there
was a riot in another football stadium, at a match between
Birmingham City and Leeds United, as a result of which a 15 year
old boy died when a wall collapsed. When we look at the horoscope

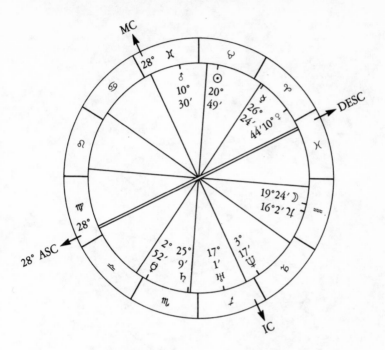

Figure 6.6 Horoscope for the Bradford football stadium fire
3.40 p.m. BST, 11 May 1985, Bradford, Yorks (53N47, 1W45)

for the fire (see Fig. 6.6) we find the familiar position of the Moon applying to a hard aspect with Saturn, having separated from a conjunction with Jupiter, and forming a T-square with the Sun. Mercury in Aries again opposes Pluto while Mars opposes Uranus.

Of the political assassinations that have shaken the world, none were more tragic than those of Abraham Lincoln in 1865 and Jack Kennedy almost 100 years later, in 1963. In the horoscope of Lincoln's assassination (see Fig. 6.7), the Sun opposes Saturn while Mercury is closely conjunct Pluto and the Moon rises in Sagittarius. At the time of Kennedy's assassination, Mercury was conjunct the Midheaven and made an extremely close applying square to Pluto, while the Moon in the 12th House applied to a conjunction with Saturn and squared Neptune (see Fig. 6.8).

Of all the atrocities perpetrated by the IRA, we can select two that gained maximum publicity for different reasons. The bombing of the Grand Hotel in Brighton in October 1984 was important because

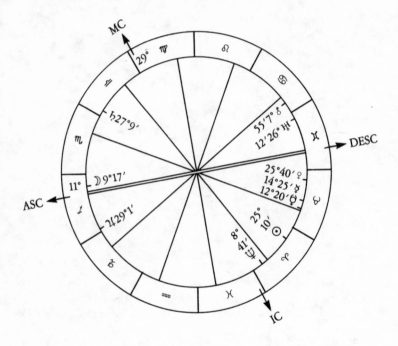

Figure 6.7 Horoscope for the assassination of Abraham Lincoln
              10.22 p.m. LT, 14 April 1865, Washington, DC (38N55, 77W00)

the entire government was almost annihilated, while the bomb attack
at Enniskillen in November 1987 was not only the worst attack in
terms of the dead and injured in a period of five years, with 11 people
killed and 61 injured, but it was particularly cold blooded, taking
place at a memorial service on Remembrance Day.

Of these two horoscopes, the latter is the more inauspicious,
bearing out the outcome in terms of human suffering. In the
horoscope of the Grand Hotel bombing, illustrated in Fig. 6.9, we

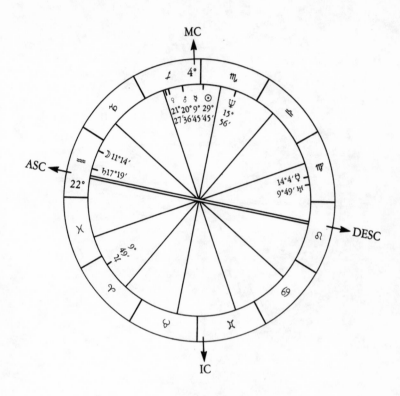

Figure 6.8 Horoscope for the assassination of President Kennedy
12.30 p.m. LT, 22 November 1963, Dallas, Texas (32N47, 96W49)

see once more the Moon applying to an opposition with Saturn, but Saturn's influence is mitigated by its application to Venus on the IC. Mars applies closely to Jupiter and is also conjunct Neptune but separating. We can contrast this horoscope with that of the Enniskillen bombing in Fig. 6.10.

In the latter horoscope the Angles are much more in evidence. The Moon again applies to an opposition with Saturn but here the orb is within one degree. Saturn rises while the Moon is close to the

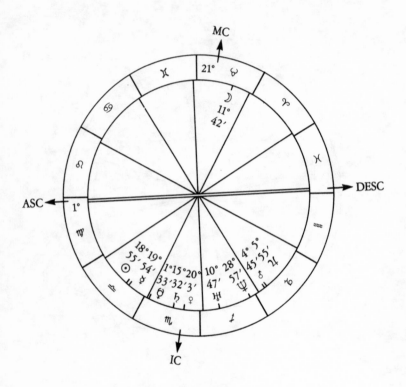

Figure 6.9 Horoscope for the bombing of the Grand Hotel
2.54 a.m. BST, 12 October 1984, Brighton, Sussex (50N50, 0W08)

Descendant and also applies to an opposition with Uranus. Mars
and Mercury are conjunct the Midheaven and both oppose Jupiter
which is exactly conjunct the IC. In addition the Sun is conjunct
Pluto in Scorpio.

The sinking of the *Herald of Free Enterprise* provides another
example of traditionally 'difficult' planets close to the Angles and
also of the differing qualities of time depending on the outer planets
being in hard aspect. During the late 1980s, Saturn, Uranus and

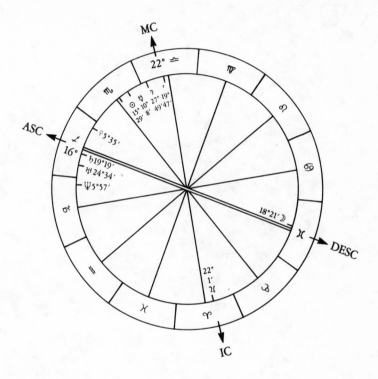

Figure 6.10 Horoscope for the Enniskillen bomb attack
          10.45 a.m. GMT, 8 November 1987, Enniskillin, Co. Fermanagh
          (54N20, 7W39)

Neptune are all close together in the latter degrees of Sagittarius
and the early degrees of Capricorn. That situation therefore governs
the whole period as the conjunction will exist in all charts throughout
the entire period. This is of course something to bear in mind when
choosing a time and it also illustrates the practical need for knowing
what to avoid. The conjunction itself cannot of course be averted
but we can ensure that it is neither in hard aspect to the Sun, Moon

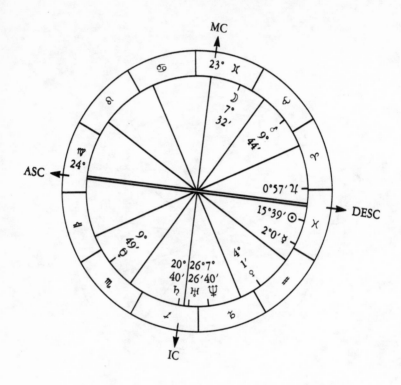

Figure 6.11 Horoscope for the sinking of the *Herald of Free Enterprise*
6.20 p.m. GMT, 6 March 1987, Zeebrugge, Belgium (51N20,
3E13)

or one of the inner planets nor close to the Angles.

In the *Herald of Free Enterprise* horoscope (see Fig. 6.11), we find
the conjunction of Saturn and Uranus straddling the IC, the latter
being at the exact mid-point of the two planets. The Moon is in
Gemini, which is appropriate for short journeys, and makes only
one hard aspect, a square to Mercury in Pisces. This configuration,
while appropriate for a ship at sea from the descriptive viewpoint,
would hardly be regarded as particularly difficult or dangerous. The
real problem area in the chart lies in the T-square which includes
an exact opposite from Mars to Pluto with both planets squaring
Venus.

By the time of the worst oilfield disaster in the world on the Piper

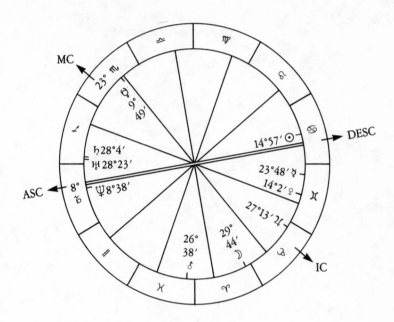

Figure 6.12 Horoscope for the Piper Alpha disaster
      9.31 p.m. BST, 6 July 1988, North Sea (Aberdeen, 57N08, 2W07)

Alpha rig in the North Sea on the evening of 6 July 1988, the conjunction of Saturn and Uranus was almost exact and in the horoscope of that event (see Fig. 6.12) we see them in the 12th House opposing Mercury and squaring Mars in Pisces. From the descriptive point of view the Moon is in Aries, signifying heat and fire, but makes no hard aspect although it is coming up to an opposition with Pluto. The explosion which blew the rig apart and killed 167 of the men on board was apparently caused by a gas leak and we find Neptune rising exactly in Capricorn opposing the Sun in Cancer.

The *Challenger* disaster, which set back the USA space programme, was described by the commander's wife as 'a horrible frozen moment in time.' We can see this frozen moment in Fig. 6.13. Pluto is close

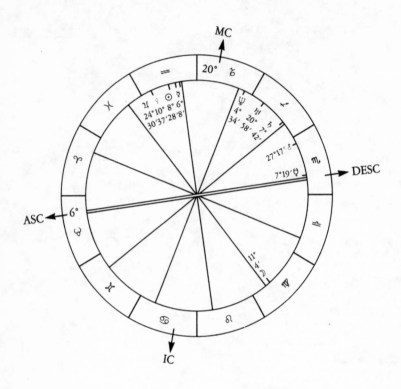

Figure 6.13 Horoscope for the *Challenger* disaster
11.38 a.m. LT, 28 January 1986, Cape Canaveral (28N30, 80W23)

to the Descendant squaring Mercury, the Sun and Venus in Aquarius.
The Moon once more squares Saturn although here it is separating
and Mars in Scorpio is square Jupiter, also in Aquarius.

To conclude this catalogue of disasters, let us look at the horoscope
of the fire that devastated the King's Cross underground station

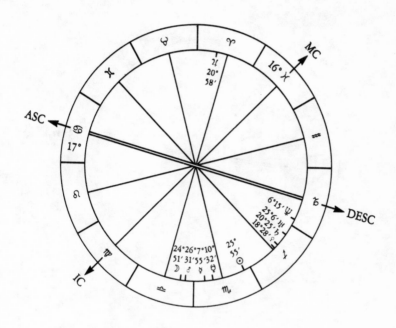

Figure 6.14 Horoscope for the King's Cross underground fire
7.20 p.m. GMT, 18 November 1987, London (51N32, 0)

(see Fig. 6.14). Starting with the Moon, we find this body in the Sign of Libra concerned with communication and closely applying to a conjunction with Mars and also separating from an opposition with Jupiter. Mercury, which rules transport, is applying to a conjunction with Pluto in Scorpio while Venus applies to the conjunction of Saturn and Uranus that we mentioned above.

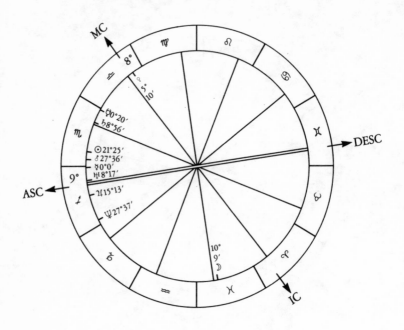

Figure 6.15 Horoscope for the arrival of Cruise missiles
           9.04 a.m. GMT, 14 November 1983, Greenham Common
           (51N25, 1W19)

The next two examples both involve women in different ways and
it is of interest to see the Moon in this context for a change. On 14
November 1983 the Cruise missiles arrived at Greenham Common.
From then on women from the various peace movements campaigned
vociferously for their removal, undergoing a great deal of abuse and
harassment in the process.

In Fig. 6.15 we find Uranus rising exactly in Sagittarius, making
a square aspect to the Moon in Pisces which is also applying to a
square with Jupiter in the 1st House. The Sun in Scorpio is applying

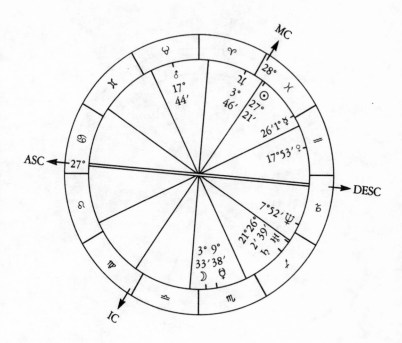

Figure 6.16 Horoscope for the first marriage ceremony in England by a
           woman
           12.15 p.m. GMT, 18 March 1987, Clifton, York (53N58, 1W07)

to a conjunction with Mars which sums up the polarity effectively.
This is an interesting chart too, which illustrates different viewpoints,
as did the chart for Hiroshima. In this horoscope, also involving the
contentious question of nuclear weapons, Jupiter and Neptune are
again in the 1st House and Venus, this time conjunct the MC, is
square Neptune.
     The first marriage ceremony to be celebrated by a woman in this
country took place on 18 March 1987. Here too, in Fig. 6.16, we have
an interesting contrast between the Sun in Pisces applying to a

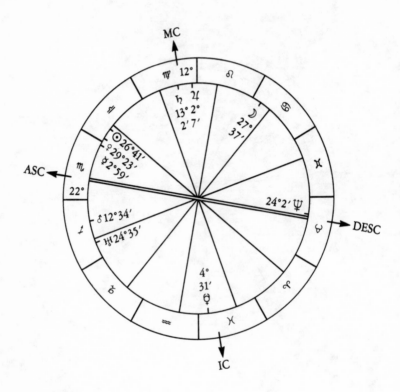

Figure 6.17 Horoscope for the Battle of Hastings
9 a.m. LMT, 14 October 1066, Battle, Sussex (50N55, 0E29)

conjunction with Jupiter on the Midheaven and squaring the Saturn–Uranus conjunction, and the Moon applying to a conjunction with Pluto in Scorpio at the bottom of the chart.

The next pair can also be read from different viewpoints, with the former leading to the latter. The chart for the battle of Hastings in 1066 (see Fig. 6.17) shows a well-placed Moon making a square aspect to the Sun, Venus and Mercury. Neptune is close to the Descendant, while Saturn is close to the Midheaven making a square

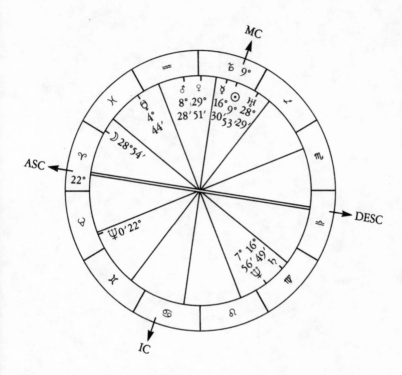

Figure 6.18 Horoscope for the coronation of William I
Noon LMT, 25 December 1066 (OS), Westminster, London
(51N30, 0W07)

aspect to Mars in the 1st House with an orb of less than one degree.

The coronation of William I (see Fig. 6.18) has Saturn replaced by the Sun on the Midheaven making a trine aspect to Jupiter and Saturn. Mercury, also close to the Midheaven, is at the apex of a Grand Trine with Neptune and Saturn. The Moon meanwhile has just passed an exact square aspect to Uranus.

This latter chart is also an inceptional horoscope, in other words one that describes the beginning of an enterprise rather than just

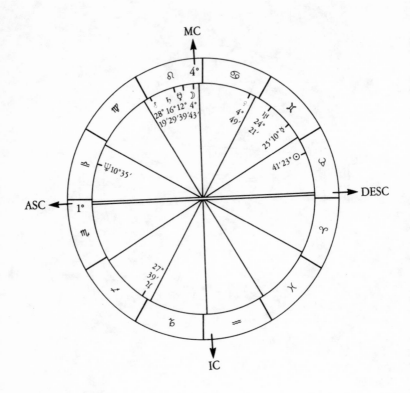

Figure 6.19 Horoscope for Israel
                4.37 p.m. LT, 14 May 1948, Tel Aviv (32N07, 34E45)

an isolated event, and it is often taken as the horoscope for Great
Britain. We may end this chapter by looking briefly at some other
charts of nations. Naturally when such a chart is chosen deliberately
it is an example of an electional chart proper and we shall examine
an example of such a chart in Part Two.

In the horoscope of Israel (see Fig. 6.19), we see an emphasis on
the Fixed Signs which include all the Angles, the Sun in Taurus,
the Moon, Midheaven and three planets placed appropriately in

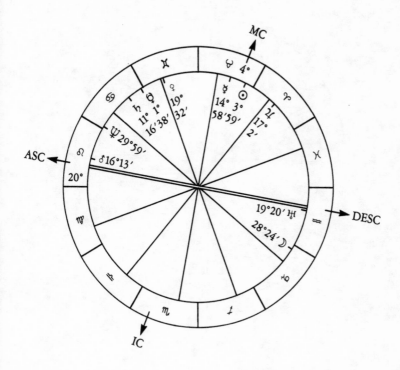

Figure 6.20 Horoscope for Eire
          Noon LT, 24 April 1916, Dublin (53N20, 6W15)

Leo. The Moon itself is very close to the Midheaven and is applying to a conjunction with Pluto, while the struggle of that hard-pressed nation can be seen in the square from the Sun to Mars.

Another nation fighting to preserve its identity is Eire, and in the chart shown in Fig. 6.20, we have Mars rising in Leo opposing Uranus exactly on the Descendant, making a T-square with Mercury in the 10th House. The Sun is also in the 10th House exactly conjunct the Midheaven, producing another T-square between the Moon in

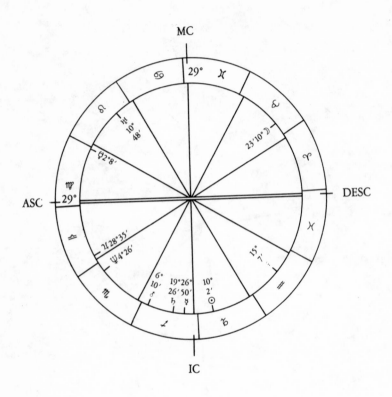

Figure 6.21 Horoscope for the European Economic Community
Midnight LT, 1 January 1958, Brussels (50N50, 4E21)

Capricorn which is applying to an opposition with Neptune.

The Moon's opposition to Neptune is also a feature in the
horoscope of the European Economic Community (see Fig. 6.21),
set up at the beginning of 1958 at midnight of 1 January. Here the
Moon is also applying to an exact square with Uranus in the 11th
House and one with Venus in the 5th House. Mercury lies close to

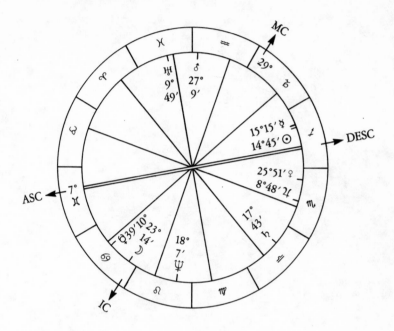

Figure 6.22 Horoscope for Northern Ireland
          3.28 p.m. LT, 7 December 1922, Belfast (54N36, 5W57)

the IC, conjunct Saturn, and Mars squares Pluto in the 12th House.

In the horoscope of Northern Ireland (see Fig. 6.22), we meet once more the familiar hard aspect between the Moon and Saturn. However, in this case the Moon is separating and the chart also includes a Grand Trine in the Water Signs between the outer planets Uranus, Pluto and Jupiter, while Neptune trines the Sun and Mercury.

PART TWO: THE PRACTICE

7.
PRELIMINARY CONSIDERATIONS

An appointed time: formulating the question
In the first half of this book I discussed the theory of electional astrology. In this half I am going to formulate the rules. Having understood how time works and how the heavenly bodies reflect the different qualities of time, we should now be in a position to choose the right time for our enterprise.

First, however, there are some preliminary matters to consider. I have emphasized throughout this book that electional astrology is different from the other branches of astrology because here alone we are creating a horoscope rather than interpreting one that is already in existence. The first consideration, therefore, is to know precisely what we are trying to achieve.

This may sound straightforward but it is of the most vital importance. Unless the aim of the enterprise is clearly formulated at the outset, we are unlikely to choose the relevant factors for its success. It is all too easy either to choose a time which is good in general according to accepted astrological principles or, alternatively, to assume a purpose which is not the real one.

A good day either in general or for one particular purpose may be entirely inappropriate for another. The Moon in Leo would certainly augur well for an outgoing event like a party or the launching of a presidential campaign, while the same body in Capricorn would dampen the most fervent exuberance and cast a sombre shadow on the festivities. But if the purpose were to achieve some practical result involving hard, deliberate work, like preparing for, or taking, an examination then the Moon's position in Capricorn would be ideal.

Equally, it is easy to make false assumptions. If we are choosing the time for a new opera production, we may be tempted to look only at Venus as the ruler of art in general and opera in particular. But is the artistic success of the production the real aim in this case?

It may or it may not be. Furthermore there may be a number of aims that need to be achieved and it will be important to be aware of these.

It is important to know the real aim of the enterprise for two reasons. First, it will affect the quality we want to provide. Do we want exuberance, discrimination, persistence, sensitivity, determination or harmony? Second, it will determine the principle that governs the enterprise. It may be artistic achievement, financial success, long-term stability or immediate expansion.

In most cases there will be a variety of aims. And becase there is a variety there will inevitably be some conflict between the different factors. This is where the complications, and the ability to weigh up and balance the needs that exist, arise in practice. Although there is real choice in electional astrology, we can only choose from the times that exist. Therefore we are not choosing an ideal time in any absolute sense, but rather the best time that is available.

That is why we need to be clearly aware of the aim or aims of the enterprise. Usually there will be one purpose which is paramount and other subsidiary objectives. It may be possible to balance these or at least the main aims, or it may be necessary to give priority to one or more of the most important.

Let us take marriage as an example. It would be natural to think of this institution in terms of love and joy. These qualities are of course of the greatest importance and no relationship would be successful without them. Physical compatibility, trust and a sense of humour are also important factors to be taken into account. But the opposing qualities, responsibility and stability, though less exciting, are as necessary if the marriage is to endure.

When we look at the real cases of successful, and indeed of unsuccessful, enterprises we can see how these principles work in practice. In a marriage which lasts beyond the initial attraction, if it is not to proceed from disillusion to dissolution, there is likely to be a combination of Saturnian influences to balance the Venusian and Jupiterian emphasis. Often Jupiter will be on the Midheaven and Saturn on the Ascendant, where social expansiveness complements personal restriction.

Having decided the purpose of the enterprise in general, the second consideration relates to its time-span. Are we trying to achieve long-term results or are we concerned with immediate success? Do we want endurance or flexibility? We may be dealing with a political election which should provide benefits beyond the moment of victory. Or we may be concerned with a race, over a in a matter of minutes.

The third consideration depends on whether the aim of the enterprise involves giving or receiving. We have looked at some length at the cycles of the heavenly bodies, especially that of the Sun. Every enterprise has its season and the ebb and flow of time correlates with its particular purpose. Here too we need to be clear as to the precise aim that we are trying to achieve.

Avoiding the difficulties that inevitably arise is in practice as important as choosing the appropriate factors. It was for this reason that I dealt in some detail with notoriously difficult times in the last chapter. There will always be potential problems at any particular time just as there are conflicts inherent in every aspect of life. As we shall see many a good horoscope has been ruined by the failure to take account or to realize the importance of problem areas. Much of the art of elections lies in a fine balance of the available factors, utilizing the positive ones while at the same time, mitigating the negative ones.

The right emphasis: understanding the alternatives

How, then, are these goals to be achieved? Let us imagine that we have been asked to select the best time for the launch of an opera company. We must first decide the purpose of the enterprise. What precisely are we trying to achieve in this particular case?

It is no use saying that opera is ruled by Venus because it is an art form and then simply ensuring that Venus is favourably placed. We must look at this specific enterprise. What are its aims? Are we looking for artistic success, financial gains, providing a long-term reputation for the performance, immediate acclamation? Are we concerned primarily about the company, the producer, the directors, the financial backers, the performers or the musicians?

Bearing in mind that in the majority of cases there will be a number of aims, we should list the main ones in order of priority. Then, if there is conflict between one or other, or if a choice has to be made because only certain qualities are available, we shall be in a position to arrange the factors in accordance with the real needs of the enterprise.

Let us assume that we are concerned, in this instance, with long-term viability rather than immediate success, with artistic acclaim to a greater extent than financial gain although we want the venture to be a commercial success. As a long-term venture we are more concerned with the management than with the stars of any particular performance.

Having listed our aims in order of priority, we need to look at the astrological correlations to see how they can be fitted in. The first practical consideration here is the time that is available. The longer the period available the wider our choice will be. With a five-year period, for example, we can look at the Signs of some of the planets. If we have only a month, on the other hand, we can only look at the Moon's position and that of the diurnal cycle. In an extreme case, with a very short period available, we may be able to do no more than avoid especially difficult areas in the chart.

Then, on the basis of the aims we have decided on for the launch of the opera company, we would first look at the ruler of the enterprise. As an art form, opera comes under the rulership of Venus which also governs financial affairs. With a combination of long-term viability and artistic acclaim as the main aims, we should look at the cycles of Saturn and Venus. As Saturn takes 29 years approximately to complete its cycle, it may not be possible to take this planet into account to any great extent. However, in principle we should look at the cycles of both these planets.

Subsidiary rulers would be the Sun for honour and acclamation and Mercury for communication. Here the question of how much time is available is of particular importance. If we have a year then we can choose any Sign, and degree, for Venus, and also for the Sun and Mercury, but not for Saturn. With only a month we would have no such choice.

Next we can select the quality of time based on our chosen aim. If we are concerned with artistic acclaim we should concentrate on Leo, for financial stability on Taurus or Capricorn, and so on. Then we should decide if we are concerned with the beginning of a cycle. Is the venture a start or a culmination or a climax? In this instance we have a launch which is clearly the beginning of a cycle and we should bear this in mind when we look at the cycles of both the Sun and the Moon.

However, we need to pause here and decide which of these factors is of the greater importance. Are we primarily concerned with the quality of the time, with the right part of the ruler's cycle, or with the question of beginning or ending? Failure to appreciate this point has in practice been the cause of many problems. All too often precedence is given to the phase of the Moon without any clear idea of the relevance of this factor.

In some cases, in planting crops, for example, the Moon's phases are of the greatest significance, but in other ventures their relevance is slight. In any event this factor will in practice conflict with others and therefore a specific choice will have to be made. If only a month is available and the Sun is in Cancer, we cannot have the Moon both in Leo and also in its Full Moon phase. So we must be sure at the outset whether the phase or the Sign of the Moon is of greater importance.

Conflicts can also arise with regard to the time of day, or the factors as they relate to the diurnal cycle. If we decide that the Moon should be in Leo, for example, and also want to place that body on the Midheaven, we will have limited our choise with regard to the Ascendant. On the other hand, by starting with the Ascendant, we automatically determine the position of the planets in the diurnal cycle.

Conflicts can never be avoided entirely. The presence of one factor will in the very process of selection affect the positions and relationships of the others. All things are connected. Similarly time, as I have stressed, is a continuum. When we choose a time in electional astrology, we do not select an isolated moment. That moment creates its own future and we should bear in mind not only where the heavenly bodies are in the electional chart itself but also where they will be as they move into the future.

8.

THE RULES OF CHOICE

In this chapter I am going to deal with the rules in so far as they relate to the electional chart itself. The first step is to decide which planet rules the enterprise, bearing in mind that the planets symbolize archetypal principles rather than the enterprise itself.

It is for this reason that I laid such stress on deciding the aim of the enterprise at the outset in the last chapter. Which planet represents the main principle or purpose of the enterprise? If necessary, we should then go on to the subsidiary aims, in strict order of importance. Having decided on the ruler, or rulers, of the enterprise in this way, we can choose the most propitious part of the planet's cycle according to the principles of cyclic astrology.

The second step is to decide on the quality we want for the enterprise. Here too we may want one quality or alternatively a variety of qualities. And here too we should list the various qualities in order of importance. Then we can arrange the relevant factors – the planets, Sun, Moon and Ascendant – in the appropriate Signs, bearing in mind that there is likely to be some conflict between the cyclic and descriptive principles.

The third step relates to the phases. Is the enterprise a beginning, a culmination or a fulfilment? Accordingly we should arrange the appropriate part of the solar, lunar and planetary phases. Finally, we must take account of the diurnal cycle, the Angles and the Houses, which relate to the mundane sphere. It is here that we can arrange for specific areas of the enterprise, such as those relating to partnerships, children or the home, for example, to be emphasized.

It is also in the diurnal cycle in particular that we can recognize potential problem areas. As we take each step in actively choosing the positive factors, we should at the same time be aware of any difficulties thrown up with regard to the Angles, the Sun, the Moon, the personal planets, and the Houses.

There are, of course, factors in the chart of which we are unaware, or the importance or meaning of which we do not appreciate. Astrology, whether we like it or not, is not an exact science. Until comparatively recently Uranus, Neptune and Pluto were unknown and so for most of its history practitioners of astrology used only five of the planets. Now Chiron has been discovered between Saturn and Uranus along with Pluto's binary, Charon, and there is a planet beyond the orbit of Pluto which is as yet unnamed and waiting to be located. Many of the fixed stars appear to have effects of varying importance, some astrologers take account of the asteroids and there are no doubt other bodies in space yet to be found.

Choosing the right time for an enterprise involves the selection of the various factors that form the tools of astrology in their strict order of importance. The final selection involves a careful balance between the different principles until the best time in the circumstances is reached. This involves an awareness of the relative weight that should be placed on these principles, and it was the lack of this appreciation, as well as the proliferation of irrelevant rules and maxims, which led to the confusion and degeneration of elections in the past.

Thus it was not so much that the rules themselves were wrong but rather that their relative importance were not recognized. The Moon's phase was given especial weight to the detriment of its placing by Sign and aspect, and, instead of deciding on the planet which ruled the enterprise according to the main aim of the venture, the ruler of the Ascending Sign was taken as the planet which governed the enterprise as a whole.

The latter error led in turn to too great an emphasis being placed on the diurnal cycle owing to the unfortunate influence of William Lilly, and the confusion with the principles of horary and natal astrology. But however muddied the waters became over the intervening centuries, the underlying principles exist and it is to these that we need to return today as we begin the practical task of creating an electional horoscope.

W.H. Auden once said: 'The great educational problem of today is how to refuse to teach people to know things before they are suffocated. For too many facts are as bad as none at all.' That is still the situation today. Electional astrology is above all a practical science and as such it is necessary to base its rules quite clearly on carefully defined principles.

The planetary principles

The first step, then, is to decide which planet or planets rule the enterprise. And therefore the first question will be: what is the primary aim of this enterprise? What is it we wish to achieve? Having established the main aim, are there any subsidiary aims? If so, what are they, and what is the order of their importance?

The planets represent archetypal principles. And it is the principles that we are concerned with here. Do we want honour, glory, material gain, justice, security, peace? Having decided on the principle we want to achieve, we then go on to choose the planet which symbolizes that principle and ensure that it is at the most appropriate part of its cycle.

What is 'its cycle'? The most important cycle in this context is the zodiacal cycle. I shall deal with the diurnal cycle, relating to the Angles and the Houses, and the synodic cycle, which relates to the planetary aspects, later in this chapter. When we look at the zodiacal cycle we see that each planetary principle functions best in general terms in certain areas of the Zodiac, not only in specific Signs but to a greater extent in particular degrees of those Signs. These are the planets' exaltations. Conversely, the opposite Signs, and degrees, are the areas where the planets are least effective in general terms. These are the falls of the planets.

Similarly each planet rules two Signs, one enabling it to function appropriately in general terms according to its yang nature and the other according to its yin nature, depending on whether the aim is to give or to receive. Again the opposite Signs are those where the planets rule only one Sign each, while the three outer planets were only discovered comparatively recently and so have not been fitted into the general pattern. It would in any event be impracticable to make a choice as to their Signs bearing in mind the time they take to circle the Zodiac.

Apart from the specific Signs of their exaltation and rulership, the planets have a greater affinity with some Signs than others. Mars, for example, as an energetic, assertive principle, will function well in the Fire Signs. However, in practice what we are looking at is a specific enterprise and therefore we must decide on the appropriateness of the planetary ruler for that particular enterprise. So, in general terms, Mars would not function at its best in Pisces but this may be the most appropriate Sign for a swimming contest.

I shall now look at the planets individually, for convenience including the Sun and Moon in that term. I shall start with the underlying principles symbolized by the planets. If we appreciate these archetypal principles we shall be able to work down the various levels of manifestation and see how they may function in a particular instance. Thus we can be aware of the possibilities with the greatest latitude. Because of its unique importance, I shall look at the Moon in a separate section.

The Sun — This body represents the primal yang power of the universe. Its principle is honour and glory, power and rulership. Heads of state or of an organization, appointments, recognition of talent, and promotion are manifestations of this principle. It is also of general significance as the god force of the universe, the male aspect of the potency which includes the Moon and the earth itself as a trinity. Therefore its position in any electional chart should be of major concern after that of the Moon.

The Sun is exalted in 19 degrees of Aries, and it rules Leo. As a yang, radiant principle it functions especially well in the Fire Signs and to a lesser extent in the Air Signs. Its cycle is a year and thus the quality of each Sign is activated for the period of a month.

Mercury — The principle of Mercury is communication. It represents the sense perceptions that enable the primal yang-yin power of the Sun and Moon to be received on Earth. Thus it too has an important general relevance in elections. From the underlying principle of communication, Mercury manifests in mental undertakings, places of learning, universities, schools and education in general. Communication also takes place of course through writing and speech, the media, television, radio, newspapers, magazines, books, public speaking, debates. And communication is brought about in the physical sense of travel, by air, sea, land and space.

Mercury is exalted in 15 degrees of Virgo and it rules, in its yang role of giving, Gemini and, in its yin role of receiving, Virgo. Here we have ideas and practical knowledge respectively. As a principle of communication it functions well in the Air Signs, while as a principle of practical learning it is appropriately placed in Capricorn as well as Virgo, but in Taurus it will meet with too much resistance. Being tied to the Sun as viewed from the earth its cycle is approximately a year.

Venus — The principle of Venus is unity, harmony, beauty. This principle, being derived from the primary yin power of the Moon, manifests as peace, harmony, justice, relationships, love, the female attribute in general and women in particular. Love and relationships lead to marriage and other forms of partnership; harmony is associated with conciliation and reconciliation; beauty and aesthetic sensibility, is associated with art, music, rhythm, style, singing, the theatre and entertainment generally. The Venus principle manifests as luxury and adornment, money and the pleasures derived from the material aspects of life.

Venus is exalted in 27 degrees of Pisces and rules, in its yang role, Libra and, in its yin role, Taurus. As the principle of love, kindness and charity it functions appropriately in Cancer as well as in Pisces, but is not well placed in the other Water Sign, Scorpio, which is its detriment. Although it rules Libra as a Sign of relationships and beauty, it is not generally well placed in the other Air Signs which are more concerned with mental attitudes and ideals. Similarly, although it functions well in Taurus as the Sign of material pleasure and sensual art forms it is not so well placed in the other Earth Signs. It too is a planet of general significance blending the power of the Sun and Moon in its unity and is also tied in its cycle to the Sun, circling the Zodiac in a period of approximately one year.

Mars — The principle of Mars is assertiveness and force. As the direct derivative of the Sun it represents the drive to reach the inner power of the individual, to break away in order to achieve one's own personality. And in opposing Venus it divides and separates and represents the male and physical sex as well as work and initiative. So it manifests as fighting in the armed forces, in competitive sports, in individual enterprise and exploration, in surgery, the police, fire brigades, butchers and crusading activities.

Mars is exalted in 28 degrees of Capricorn and rules, in its yang role, Aries and, in its yin role, Scorpio. As an outgoing, forceful energy it functions well in all the Fire Signs. Although it is exalted in Capricorn, it does not function so well in the other Earth Signs, especially Taurus which is its detriment, nor does it find the Water Signs, apart from Scorpio, congenial. Its cycle is two years and thus each Sign is activated for a period of two months. As the furthest personal planet from the Earth it too is important as a general principle, though less so than the closer bodies.

Jupiter — The principle of Jupiter is co-operation, construction, hierarchy. Whereas Mars breaks down, Jupiter builds up in the widest sense. It is therefore the organization, the unity which produces the first tangible form in the material world that is symbolized by this planet. The structure and the outer limits of this form then come under the rulership of the next planet, Saturn. So any body which is built up as an organization, whether it be a government, a religion, a judiciary, will be governed by Jupiter. Thus a community or group which represents the principle of teamwork or brotherhood, a trade union or a university in its corporate establishment, for example, will come under this planet.

And, because it governs the form of an organization in its active nature, it also rules the physical structure of the body built up. It is important therefore to appreciate the distinction between the purpose and the structure of the enterprise when deciding initially on the primary aim. So, for example, in horse racing, the race itself would be ruled by Mars while the racing establishment and the course would be ruled by Jupiter. Similarly, in the case of education, the teaching would be ruled by Mercury, while the university establishment would be ruled by Jupiter.

Jupiter is exalted in 15 degrees of Cancer. It rules, in its yang role, Sagittarius and, in its yin role, Pisces. As an expansive, outgoing principle it functions best in the Fire Signs and to a lesser extent in the Air Signs. It also functions reasonably well in the two Water Signs, Cancer and Pisces, where its generosity and optimism are expanded, but not in Scorpio. The Earth Signs, on the other hand, provide less ability for its growth. Its cycle is 12 years and thus each Sign is activated for one year.

Saturn — The principle of Saturn is order and restraint. While Jupiter represents constructive building, Saturn symbolizes the limits and restrictions as well as the material foundations of an enterprise. Here too it is important to appreciate the underlying principle of this planet for its material manifestations may easily be confused with those of Jupiter even though in theory the principles are opposites. Jupiter, for instance, represents the constructive side of religion, the law and government, the sense of love, justice and equality manifesting in practical shape. Saturn, on the other hand, represents the restraining side of these bodies, the outer forms. In practice Saturn manifests in the land, the Civil Service, prisons, mental hospitals, mining, national boundaries and frontiers.

Saturn is exalted in 21 degrees of Libra. It rules, in its yang role, Aquarius and, in its yin role, Capricorn. It functions best in the Earth

Signs and least well in the Fire Signs. Its cycle is approximately 29 years and so it activates each Sign for about two years.

The three outer planets were only discovered comparatively recently and therefore do not fit into the traditional scheme of things. In practice it will not usually be possible to arrange them in an appropriate Sign, nor do they have exaltations or falls and they rule only one Sign. However, their principles are important and I shall mention them briefly here.

Uranus — The principle of Uranus is change which manifests in discovery and revolution. It rules inventions, science in the sense of new understanding and the drive to be different. It rules Aquarius and its cycle is 84 years, thus activating each Sign for seven years.

Neptune — The principle of Neptune is perfection and completeness. It manifests through the imagination, the spiritual, the sense of oneness that may be achieved in art or in the care and sacrifice that embraces humanity as a whole. It can also manifest as the attempt to escape from the confines of material reality into a world of illusion or delusion, such as through drugs or alcohol. Thus it rules the spiritual aspect of religion, the esoteric arts in general, hypnotism, anaesthetics, fraud, spying, the cinema, the sea, oil and all that is hidden. It rules Pisces and its cycle is 165 years, thus remaining in each Sign for approximately 14 years.

Pluto — The principle of Pluto is renewal. It manifests explosively, building up from hidden depths. It rules death and rebirth, volcanoes, eruptions, mass murder, psychiatry and pathology. It rules Scorpio and its cycle is 250 years and thus remains in each Sign for approximately 20 years.

The orbit of the Moon

I am going to look at the Moon separately because of its unique position in electional astrology. While in principle it operates in the same way as the other heavenly bodies, the Sun and the planets, as a matter of degree, and therefore of practice, its importance is equivalent to all these factors put together. Indeed if our time-span is short, a matter of only a few days, we can concentrate almost entirely on the Moon's position.

There are five important functions of the Moon: first, its specific principle according to the cyclic approach; second, its general principle in elections; third, its reflection of a particular quality of time according to the descriptive approach; fourth, the modification of these qualities according to its aspects; fifth, the phases of the Moon. Let us look at these in turn.

First is the Moon's specific principle according to the cyclic approach. The principle of the Moon is change, receptiveness, fluctuation. Just as the Sun represents the primal, yang, outgoing, male force of the universe, so the Moon represents the primal yin or female power. Women in general and mothers in particular come under the Moon's rulership. It also rules the people as a whole and the institution of democracy in contrast to those in authority who come within the ambit of the Sun.

The Moon is exalted in 3 degrees of Taurus and it rules the Sign of Cancer. Because of its association with love and caring it also functions well in Pisces. In theory it should be well placed in the yin as opposed to the yang Signs, but in practice Scorpio is the Sign of its fall while Capricorn is that of its detriment. The precision of Virgo will also find difficulty in accommodating the natural flow of the Moon's currents and fluctuations.

The Moon's affinity with people as a whole brings us to its second function, or its general principle in elections. The unique importance of the Moon arises because of its physical proximity to the earth. As the only satellite of our planet it is not only far closer than any other body but it acts as a focus for the Sun and the other bodies in the sky. Thus its position is peculiar to the earth and reflects the affairs of our world in a way more immediate than the other factors.

It is for this reason that the Moon rules the mundane sphere as a whole and here its specific rulerships are subsumed in a wider application. And because the Moon rules affairs on earth in general its relative importance is great. In particular the Moon reflects the power of the Sun and is the goddess, as opposed to the god. So the Sun symbolizes the spirit while the Moon represents the soul, the mediator between heaven and earth. Therefore it also rules the astral plane and magic.

Third is the descriptive role of the Moon. As we have seen, according to this principle, the quality of a particular time is described by the Sign which is being activated by one of the heavenly bodies for the period that body is passing through that Sign. Therefore, as the Moon passes through all the Signs of the Zodiac in one month, each Sign will be activated for a period of approximately two and a half days.

In theory this period is but another time just as the position of the Sun through the Signs determines the seasons and the earth's rotation the run of the hours. But in practice the quality of any particular time is described in its most immediate sense by the Moon's position. Thus here too the Moon assumes an importance far greater than any other heavenly body. While we can use the Sun's position to choose the general tenor of a month, if we want a day of exuberance, radiating power and warmth we should select a day when the Moon is in Leo.

Fourth is the modification of these qualities according to the aspects. This is the second element of the descriptive approach, for the underlying quality of the day will vary depending on the aspects made to the Moon. I shall look at the aspects themselves later in this chapter. At this stage I shall deal with the principles involved.

Much confusion has been caused in the past by the failure to appreciate the degree of importance as well as the practical application of the various aspects. The traditional rules state that the Moon should be as well aspected as possible, and Ptolemy even goes so far as to say that it is ideal to place the Moon in good aspect to all the planets that rule the business. Strictly speaking there is nothing incorrect about these statements. If it were possible then certainly a well-aspected Moon could only be beneficial.

However, the emphasis in these statements is wrong. If we start by trying to arrange 'good' aspects to the Moon we shall be limiting our range of choice considerably. This is particularly important as the beneficial aspects have very little effect in practice. Because electional astrology is a branch of mundane astrology, we are concerned with bringing situations into manifestation. The aspects therefore which are relevant are the hard aspects and in practice the major ones, i.e. the conjunction, square and opposition.

Thus the situation in elections is that these hard aspects from Pluto, Neptune, Uranus, Saturn, Jupiter and Mars to the Moon will produce qualities according to the nature of those planets which then modify the underlying quality described by the Moon's Sign. Furthermore, the way these planetary qualities are brought into manifestation is through the application of the Moon towards the aspect. So as the Moon applies to a hard aspect the quality begins to manifest, starting a day before exactitude. The climax then takes place at exactitude, and once that point is passed the effect is over.

Although these hard aspects can be used constructively, they are more likely to produce difficulties. The basic rule therefore is to avoid applying hard aspects to the Moon. Indeed, if we have only a very short period of time for our choice, we should at least try to ensure that the Moon is not in hard aspect to the outer planets. Adhering to this rule and keeping difficult planets away from the Angles will to a great extent avert major disasters.

The fifth important function is the phases of the Moon. The phases of the Moon are of course the aspects of that body to one other body, the Sun. And just as there has been much confusion engendered by the old rules with regard to aspects in general, so in the case of the Moon's phases the traditional rules have provided a totally misleading emphasis.

Robson, for example, states: 'As in all branches of astrology, a good aspect between the Moon and the Sun is an excellent foundation for success, and will improve any election.'[1] In itself this statement is incontrovertible. However, he then goes on to say that such an aspect will make all the difference between success and failure. This has led to astrologers using a trine aspect between the Moon and the Sun as the starting point of an electional chart. The result has usually been disastrous. While it is true that a soft aspect between these two bodies is beneficial, the relative importance of such an aspect is small, and the practical results of starting with such an aspect has meant that other, more important, factors cannot be utilized.

So what is the importance of the Moon's phases in elections? Let us first be clear what these symbolize. Because the Sun and the Moon represent the two primary forces of the universe, the yang and the yin, and because the Moon acts as a focus for the Sun's power, it combines in its phases the power of both bodies. That is why the Moon's phases are of particular importance in magical ceremonies which depend on the relative potency of the yin and the yang forces, the goddess and the god.

So far as electional astrology is concerned, the relevance of the Moon's phases is twofold. The first relates to the periods which divide the month into two, while the second relates to the separate phases. With regard to the first, the period from the New to the Full Moon is the yang half of the cycle, while the period from the Full Moon to the New is the yin half, or the waxing and waning phases respectively. These are analogous to the two halves of the solar cycle from spring to autumn and back to spring again. If the enterprise is one which involves building up or creating then the waxing phase is appropriate, but if it involves pulling down or destroying then the waning phase should be chosen.

These two periods can then be broken down into the separate phases and it is here that the aspectual nature of the Sun and Moon can most clearly be seen. We can also see how the traditional rules translate time into space when we look at Fig. 8.1. Traditionally it

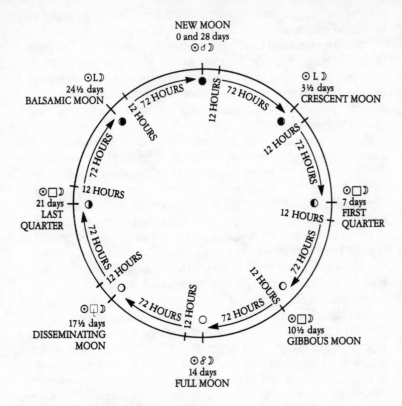

Figure 8.1 Time and space in the lunar cycle

is said that the first 12 hours from the exact time of the New Moon
are bad, while the next 72 are good, the next 12 are bad, the following
72 beneficial and so on. These periods of 12 hours represent an orb
of about 6½ degrees following the hard aspects, including here the
semi-squares and sesquiquadrates as well as the conjunctions, squares
and oppositions, bearing out the general difficulties involved in these
hard aspects.

The diurnal cycle: the Angles and the Houses
The diurnal cycle – the choice of the Angles, which determine the
Houses – grounds the enterprise. The Ascendant is important as
the immediate starting point of the enterprise and the Angles as
a whole are powerful points in the electional chart which attract the
seeds of conflict, danger and challenge. The Houses show where
specific events occur in the mundane sphere.

Two principles co-exist in the diurnal cycle. First, the Angles and the Houses represent the enterprise according to its mundane circumstances. This principle is analogous to natal, and indeed mundane, astrology. So the Ascendant represents the immediate perception, or image, of the enterprise, the way it appears and comes across in its physical manifestation. The Descendant defines its approach to others, its projections, attractions and relationships, while the Midheaven shows its aspirations in the world at large and the way it will function in that realm, and the IC reflects its roots and foundations together with the conditions of its early environment.

The Houses symbolize the spheres of material manifestation as they do in the other branches of astrology. So the 9th House represents the vision of the enterprise, the dreams that will manifest in the concrete realm of the 10th House, and thus the philosophy, the wider horizons, the outreaching exploration of the venture which may materialize in mundane terms in the form of higher learning or long journeys.

On the basis of this principle, we can choose either to place an appropriate planet in one of the Houses, or alternatively ensure that a planet is not in a particular House. In the foundation of a school, for example, we may be especially concerned about the 5th House which represents creativity, offspring, works of art and children. So on the one hand we might want to place Mercury in that House, while on the other, if Mars were badly aspected, we might wish deliberately to exclude it from that area of the chart.

The second principle concerns the Ascendant as the focus for the chart as a whole. It is with regard to this principle that great care needs to be taken, for much confusion has been caused by the failure to understand the real nature of the principle. The Ascendant is the point of immediate contact with the environment as the Sun rises over the horizon. Thus the Sign on the Ascendant provides the quality for the beginning of the enterprise, its most immediate quality.

Unfortunately, on the analogy of horary astrology, far too great, and incidentally a false, emphasis has been placed on this one factor. Because the Ascendant symbolizes the beginning of the venture, it is taken to represent the venture as a whole. However, this analogy is not valid for elections. In elections, as in some other branches of astrology, the Ascendant has a role in time and space. As a factor in time, it reflects the way the enterprise starts, its immediate beginning. As a factor in space, it indicates how the enterprise comes across, or appears, in its most immediate form.

Now in elections the starting point is one factor among many. Furthermore, the degree of its importance will depend on the kind of enterprise. We have seen from the descriptive viewpoint that the Ascendant reflects the quality of the Sign it is in for a period of approximately two hours, while the Moon shows the quality of its Sign for about two and a half days and the Sun for a month. It is the Moon which symbolizes the main qualities of an enterprise while the Sun and the personal planets have important secondary roles to play.

The Ascendant too has an important role to play but its position needs to be seen in the context of the factors as a whole. If the beginning of the enterprise is of particular concern, where, for example, a space probe is being launched, then it will assume a greater importance. Where a city is being founded, on the other hand, the primary concern is for long-term stability rather than immediate results, and in this case the main importance of the Ascendant would centre on the mundane sphere in its role as the most potent Angle.

In horary astrology, on the other hand, the only concern is to answer a specific question. 'Where is Lady Mountjoy's ring?' The moment this question is asked, or received, constellates the heavens so that the answer can be read according to the exact moment which is symbolized in the Ascendant. So, in this branch, the rising point assumes supreme importance and the planet which governs the enterprise as a whole is the one which rules the rising Sign.

The answers sought in horary astrology are also precise. Where exactly on Lord Seaford's estate did Lady Mountjoy lose her ring? And as the answers are precise, so are the roles of the Houses specific. For if the ruler of the 2nd House of property is in the 5th conjunct Neptune, and Virgo is on the cusp of the 5th, we may assume that the ring has been swallowed by a playful chicken.

However, in elections we are neither concerned with answering questions nor are we dealing with specifics. In elections the Ascendant, and the Angles as a whole, are part of the continuum of time – time that never ceases and that reflects the pattern of life as it moves through its cycles. The Houses are important in elections if we want to avoid a problem, or even be aware of its existence, or if we want to emphasize a particular area of the mundane cycle. Neptune in a marriage chart suggests delays or confusion but that planet has to be placed somewhere. In the 3rd House the principle would apply to brothers and sisters, and short journeys. In the author's wedding chart, Neptune was placed in that position as it was impossible to arrange anything more propitious. At least there was the benefit of foreknowledge when the bride's sister arrived late and in tears, having got lost in the one-way traffic system.

And in elections it is usually more appropriate to look at the Angles, and indeed at the diurnal cycle as a whole, in a wider context. According to the traditional rules, it is stated that the power of the planets depends on whether they are in Angular, Succedent or Cadent Houses, and furthermore that a planet is most powerful in an Angular House, less powerful in a Succedent House, and incapable of effecting much one way or the other in a Cadent House.

It is worth while at this point to ensure that we are aware of the real meaning and principle of the diurnal cycle. The diurnal cycle orientates the planets so that they are brought within the compass of our lives on earth. The orientation itself is determined by the two axes, horizontal and vertical, which define our approach towards ourselves, each other, our social and spiritual needs and our environment. These two axes form the four Angles and it is these that create the cross which is the symbol of the earth and our existence in this incarnation. Here the circle is squared and time is shaped from eternity.

The exact breakdown of the Houses within the Angles is therefore of secondary importance and in any event can never be exactly defined with no agreed basis of House division. In practical terms we should regard the four quarters of the chart as beginning at one of the Angles and gradually decreasing in power as they leave one Angle and approach the next.

We can therefore retain the principle of Angular, Succedent and Cadent Houses while changing the emphasis. The closer to the Angles, the more actively potent a planet will be. As it moves towards the middle of the quadrant, the more concentrated and stable will be its power, and then as it moves towards the next Angle the more flexible and correspondingly less powerful it will become. As it approaches the following Angle, it regains its active power. The actual side of the Angle is unimportant in terms of potency. What matters is the proximity of the planet to the Angle.

The relative importance of the diurnal cycle is a matter of great importance in practice because it determines the way this cycle is used. Electional astrology involves a process of active selection between different principles which are likely to conflict. Therefore a wrong starting point or a false emphasis on one factor will mean that other factors are not given the emphasis they deserve. It is in this realm in particular that electional astrology has failed to fulfil its promise so far.

Although the Angles and Houses are of great importance in elections they do not hold the position of supreme importance that they do in horary astrology. Moreover it is necessary to judge each election on its individual merits to decide how important any particular factor is. As a general rule, however, the overall quality of the enterprise is determined primarily by the Moon while the planet which governs the enterprise is that which represents the real principle behind the enterprise. The Ascendant, on the other hand, is the starting point for the venture, and the Houses show where particular situations will occur.

Making choices in elections is rather like arranging the colours and shapes in an abstract painting. All things are connected. Each will affect its neighbour and the relationship between the factors as a whole. As an initial consideration, it is necessary to appreciate that these choices do have to be made deliberately. Starting with the Ascendant rather than the position of the Moon, for example, in itself limits subsequent choices.

So if we begin by deciding that we want a chart with Aries rising and make that our starting point, we have already determined the positions of most of the planets in the Houses, depending on the time-span involved. On the other hand, if our primary consideration is to ensure that the Moon is in Leo conjunct the Midheaven we will have thereby limited our choice of Ascendant.

Sometimes the choice will be relatively simple. On other occasions we will need to balance one factor against another and perhaps arrive at a compromise when there is no ideal time. This in itself involves the need to appreciate the relative importance of the various factors. So if we want the Moon in Leo conjunct the Midheaven, there may be a problem with a Scorpio Ascendant, enhanced by the position of Pluto closely conjunct the rising point. In that case the answer may be to move the Moon a little farther into the 10th House and have Libra rising.

There are also two other aspects of the diurnal cycle which I have touched on and which go back to the old magical principles. First, the day has its own cycle analogous to the seasons of the Sun and the monthly phases of the Moon. Just as the solar year begins with spring and progresses through its first cross-quarter day in the middle of May to the culmination of the summer solstice in June, so the day begins at dawn and reaches a cross-point at 9 a.m. and then high noon at midday when it proceeds through an analogous cycle. So from dawn to dusk it is a yang time when beginnings are made, while the latter half of the cycle from dusk to dawn is the yin period when it is time for receptive endeavours.

Finally, there are the planetary hours which form part of a cycle depending on the relative distance of these bodies from the earth. As we have seen, each planet rules one hour just as it rules one day of the week and its own longer period of time. Here too a choice must be made, for if our starting point is to be based on the appropriate planetary hour any independent choice of Ascendant will be precluded.

Signs and seasons

'Do it when the Moon is in Scorpio.' Medieval astrology was full of such forthright, if ambiguous, statements, which were based on the assumption that to engage in a particular activity one particular Sign would be appropriate.

So what do the Signs of the Zodiac represent in electional astrology? The Signs reflect the quality of a particular time. The Zodiac as a whole is the underlying web of time that constitutes the temporal dimension of life, that changes from moment to moment, from month to month, from year to year, from age to age as the heavenly bodies weave their patterns and leave their images on the window of eternity.

The Signs therefore reveal the general backdrop of time. Each has its own quality. As the Sun, the Moon, the planets and the earth itself move in time, the qualities inherent in the Signs are brought out. And as the heavenly bodies create patterns of relationships between each other the nature of the individual Signs is affected – interfused, blended, mingled.

We have seen that we can look at the planetary bodies from either the cyclic or the descriptive viewpoint. According to the cyclic viewpoint, we choose the planet which rules the enterprise, and then place it in the area of the Zodiac which corresponds most appropriately with its cycle. According to the descriptive viewpoint, we decide on the most appropriate quality for the enterprise and then place one of the heavenly bodies in the Sign which reflects that quality.

The function of the Signs themselves, however, is the same whichever viewpoint is taken. When we place the Sun, Moon or one of the planets in one of the Signs we are activating the quality reflected by that Sign. The difference in the two viewpoints lies in their purpose. If we take the cyclic viewpoint, then we are ensuring that the quality chosen is the most appropriate for the planet ruling the enterprise. If, on the other hand, we take the descriptive viewpoint, we concentrate on the general quality that is appropriate for the enterprise.

So much for the theory. In practice we begin by looking at the ruler or rulers of the enterprise. In which Sign or, if necessary, degree should the ruling planet be placed? In this case it is the appropriate Sign according to the general nature of the planetary cycle that is being considered. Here we look at the general and at the particular circumstances according to the planetary ruler. According to general principles, Mercury is exalted in Virgo and rules both that Sign and also Gemini. Should either of those Signs, or alternatively one more suitable to the particular purpose, be chosen for the launching of a space probe?

Next a decision needs to be made on the quality of the enterprise. Is it to be intensity, endurance, exuberance, calm, versatility? In order to arrange the necessary quality, the appropriate body is placed in the Sign which reflects that quality. Here the Moon is by far the most important body and symbolizes the overall quality of the enterprise. The inceptional quality is reflected in the rising Sign, while the sun and the planets reflect the longer periods of time.

Having made these decisions we have only to choose the right Sign for the various heavenly bodies. To appreciate the nature of the Signs for the purposes of elections, I shall look at them first as a whole and then individually.

Taking the Signs as a whole to begin with, we can look first at their division into the two opposing energies: the yin and the yang, or negative and positive currents. These opposing energies are relevant in two ways. The alternate yin/yang current through the Signs is the one with which we are most familiar. This is like an electric current where the first Sign, Aries, is yang or positive, the second, Taurus, is yin or negative, the third, Gemini is yang and so on through the entire cycle of the Zodiac.

In addition, the first half of the cycle, from Aries to Virgo, is the yang half, while the second, from Libra to Pisces, is the yin. This is the seasonal approach, where the year and all other cycles is divided into a waxing and waning phase. So the yang period is the time for initiation, for sowing and creating, while the yin is the time for fulfilment, reaping and reflection.

The next division produces the four Elements. Here we have the general qualities of the Signs according to the four principle methods of alignment. The Fire Element reflects action and enthusiasm, the Air communication and rational thought, the Water sensitivity, the way of the emotions, while the practical, constructive approach is represented by the Earth Element.

The third division produces the three Modes. These govern the speed of the enterprise. The Cardinal Signs, as the initiators of the seasons, are the fastest and therefore in general they are best for a speedy conclusion. The Fixed Signs represent the concentration of power and are therefore appropriate where the aim is endurance and long-term stability. The Mutable Signs are the most flexible and therefore most appropriate where change is desired. In practice the Mutable Signs are only rarely an appropriate choice for they have neither the quality of endurance nor the force of a strong start.

We can now look at the Signs individually. Because the universe is a whole, the quality that is reflected in a Sign pervades all facets of existence. It can be felt in the general atmosphere of the day or other period of time, it can be recognized in the weather, and it will be apparent in the events that occur and that are thrown out of the pattern of time. The best way to experience the different qualities of the Signs is to be aware of the Moon's passage through each Sign during the course of a month. I shall illustrate the nature of the Signs briefly by looking first at their overall quality and then at ways in which they may manifest in elections.

Aries — Aries is the fastest Sign. The Cardinal Signs as a whole are appropriate for initiating but in practice there is a great difference between the speed of Aries and Capricorn, for example. Action, movement, speed are the qualities of this Sign. It is a time when it is difficult to be still and the energy generated should be utilized and channelled into an outgoing venture.

The weather will be sunny, bright and bracing with a combination of warmth and movement in the atmosphere. This will be the most appropriate Sign for getting an enterprise off to a good start, and for a fast beginning. The quality will be right for forceful endeavours, such as racing, fighting and taking risks. But because of the sense of restlessness there is likely to be danger on the roads; impetuous behaviour will mean lack of consideration for others and it will be an inappropriate time for sustained endeavour, hard work and enterprises that are concerned with endurance and stability.

Taurus — By way of contrast, Taurus is the slowest Sign. It is stable, dependable, enduring. The atmosphere will be heavy and full, sensual and rich, filled with the fragrance of nature, ripe with earth's promise, like an awakening bud. Because of its heavy fullness it is the wettest Sign after those of the Water Element. It is excellent for long-term ventures, founding a city, a business or a bank, and also for pleasurable activities where time is not of the essence. An enterprise founded under the influence of Taurus will last but it is not a sign conducive to speed or excitement.

Gemini — Gemini is light, versatile, communicative and flexible. The atmosphere will be restless but stimulating, and the weather windy, usually dry but with occasional light showers interspersed by scattered bright sunshine. It is a good time for coming into contact with other people, for discussions, writing, publishing, learning, travelling, involvement in the media and journalism. It is not an appropriate time, however, for more lasting endeavours as the initial enthusiasm is unlikely to be sustained.

Cancer — Cancer is protective and sheltering. Its atmosphere is emotional and receptive. The weather reflected by its quality will be wet and the rain persistent. Although it is a Cardinal Sign its initiation will be conservative and its enterprise slow, its achievement reflecting that of the tortoise rather than the hare. It is a good for building secure parameters, and for activities concerned with caring and nurturing, whether they be human, educational, spiritual or in business. Thus it is an appropriate Sign for building houses, institutions, hospitals and schools but not for enterprises involving risk.

Leo — Leo is radiant and enthusiastic. There is a sense of grandeur and optimism, a feeling that success is imminent, and a general quality of well-being. The atmosphere is hot, glowing like a cat basking in front of a fire. It is an excellent time for enterprises that concern leadership, or for propagating a visionary idea that will enthuse people whether through the arts or by some form of dramatic speech. Whenever confidence is needed for an endeavour, in the founding of a new state, for example, this Sign should be in evidence. It is not so good for concentrated, intense activities or where a quick, forceful start is required.

Virgo — Virgo is careful and discriminating. The general atmosphere is anxious, with an underlying nervous sensibility and tension. Tempers can get frayed and there is a temptation to be critical and pedantic. The weather is changeable, slightly disturbed, often cloudy with some light rain and generally dull. It is a good time for being involved in detailed, practical endeavours, and excellent for teaching and for concentrated activities, from revision courses for examinations to gardening. It is not a good time for activities which are more outgoing and where decisiveness is important. While it can be the best Sign for the Moon with regard to certain enterprises, it is usually very difficult as a rising Sign and is commonly in that position in the charts of major disasters.

Libra — Libra is a Sign of active communication. Its atmosphere is vibrant and extrovert. The weather will be windy but dry, with a vital, bracing quality, although often the winds will be strong. It is an excellent time for the exchange of ideas, and for beginning an enterprise where people and ideals are central. With an innate sense of rhythm and flow, endeavours concerned with social and artistic elements are emphasized. Opening an art gallery or an opera house, forming a new television channel, or inaugurating a telecommunications service would come under this influence.

Scorpio — This is the most intense of the Signs. The atmosphere will be deep, with a sense of some subterranean power moving towards the surface. The weather is wet, the rain relentless, or cold and biting. It is a good time for concentrated hard work especially where discoveries need to be made in the deeper layers of a project, where the depths can be probed for new insights. Research projects, investigations, and involved financial and business ventures would all benefit from these qualities.

Sagittarius — Sagittarius, by way of contrast, is active, outgoing, exploring. There is a sense of movement, of excitement even, and of adventure. The weather is boisterous, windy but usually sunny and warm. It is a good time for discovery, travel and for any endeavour where horizons need to be widened and new ideas accepted. Sporting activities, higher learning and space exploration would be appropriate when this Sign is activated.

Capricorn — There is a certain paradox about this Sign. Although it is a Cardinal Sign and so good for starting an enterprise, in terms of speed its pace is as slow as Taurus. Delays are frequent when the Moon is in Capricorn, and the world in general, and transport in particular, appears to proceed in slow motion. Yet Capricorn is relentless and will make up for its slow start by dogged persistence. The atmosphere in general is gloomy with a sense of impending doom in the air. The weather will be overcast, grey, cloudy with a fine, insistent drizzle. It is a good time for study and hard work, constructive building, inaugurating a business project or buying land. It is definitely not a good time for inspiring enthusiasm or launching an exciting venture.

Aquarius — Aquarius emphasizes new ideas and technology, communicating principles and discoveries. The atmosphere is bright and still; there will be little movement and sometimes a slight chill in the air. It is good for broadcasting, propagating ideas in education, politics and social affairs, through journalism, books or the media. As a Fixed Sign, long-term success in these fields is stressed and founding a publishing company, newspaper, or a company concerned with new technology would be appropriate.

Pisces — This is the most sensitive and receptive of the Signs. The general atmosphere is enervative with a sense of lassitude and tiredness. It is the wettest of all the Signs, exaggerated by windy conditions. It is also a very emotional time when tears are close to the surface. It is good for caring endeavours, in particular humanitarian enterprises involving the mentally ill, the handicapped and those in need. It is also good for spiritual and esoteric activities, artistic and poetic ventures, and things connected with the sea or the brewery trade. However, with the combination of confusion due to over-sensitivity and excessive flexibility, it is not good for practical endeavours generally and is not inclined to great stability or endurance.

Aspects and phases
So far we have been concerned with arranging the separate factors of the horoscope in the right areas of the Zodiac and the diurnal cycle. We have started by choosing the planet which rules the enterprise, ensuring that this is in the most appropriate Sign and, if necessary, House. We have found the best quality for the day by getting the Moon and, to a lesser extent, the Sun, Mercury, Venus and Mars in the most compatible Sign and House.

Now we need to see the pattern as a whole. Let us be clear at the outset what the aspects mean. While the Sun, Moon and planets describe the underlying quality of time by activating the Signs they are in, the aspects define the relationship between these separate factors. More specifically, the aspects modify the underlying quality of the Signs which is brought out by the Sun, Moon and planets. It is convenient to think of this process in two stages.

If the Moon is in Cancer, the day will be emotional, sensitive, caring. If Mars squares the Moon, there will be emotional assertiveness, anger, irritation. Tempers may be lost, relationships are liable to be fraught. On the other hand, if Mars squares the Moon in Aries, the underlying quality will be direct, outgoing, vibrant. In this situation therefore the assertiveness will be direct and outgoing. So there may be physical violence, accidents owing to excessive speed, and recklessness because risks are taken without care or foresight.

I have made the point already in this book that the success of elections depends to a large extent on being selective. There is an almost limitless number of factors that could be taken into consideration and much of the confusion in the present state of elections lies in the fact that insufficient weight is given to certain factors while too much is given to others. Nowhere is this more true than in the area of the aspects.

First, then, which aspects are important in electional astrology? In elections we are primarily concerned with what is happening in the material world. We want our enterprise to succeed in practical terms, whether it is a space probe or the founding of a political party. The aspects that relate to happenings on the material level are the hard ones and therefore as a matter of practice it is these which are of the greatest importance. The soft aspects relate to ease of accomplishment, a passive state of facility rather than any actual achievement. It is beneficial to have an easy aspect between planets but the relative importance of these is slight. Moreover, as such a choice usually means sacrificing one factor for another, it is far more important to avoid difficulties than to provide some slight measure of ease.

In practical terms, therefore, the aspects which are important in elections are the conjunction, the square and the opposition. Only if it is possible to arrange for the introduction of a trine or sextile, without also creating one of the hard aspects elsewhere, should the soft ones be used.

Second, how is the nature of the planets themselves brought out by the aspects? In traditional astrology we read of 'avoiding aspects with malefics' as well as 'fortifying the ruling planet'. The concept of 'malefics' and 'benefics' is of course a simplistic, not to say a misleading one. The fact is that each planet represents a specific principle and this principle can function both positively and negatively. Any planet in its own way – Jupiter as much as Saturn – can create problems when in aspect with the personal factors in an electional chart. Equally, any planet can provide the qualities needed for a particular enterprise.

Third, how do the aspects operate in elections? As opposed to natal astrology, it is not just a question of a planet being in aspect with another. In natal astrology we are looking at a static picture and it is this that we interpret. In electional astrology we are looking at an enterprise which develops in time. Here we are concerned with the moving cycles of the planets, as they approach each other, reach an exact aspect and then separate in order to continue their cycles and form further aspects with each other.

We have seen that for the underlying quality of time we should look at the Moon's position by Sign. That quality is then modified by the planets in aspect to the Moon. The hard aspects have the greatest effect while the soft aspects, to a limited extent, produce a sense of ease. The Moon passes through the whole Zodiac in a month and therefore it will make a hard aspect to each planet approximately once a week and will run through the whole range of aspects each month.

The effects of a hard aspect with the Moon can be felt first about a day before exactitude. Gradually the pressure increases and the contact becomes more potent until exactitude is reached. Then the effects are over and the next aspect begins to be formed. The degree of potency of any aspect is related to the proximity, or orb, of the aspect. The other aspects which are important in practice are those to the Sun, Mercury, Venus and Mars and once again the potency of these will increase as the orbs decrease.

The mutual aspects between the outer planets operate on a different timescale. There is usually no question of deliberately choosing an aspect between Pluto and Saturn but it is important to appreciate these aspects as part of the overall pattern that exists in the sky at any time. So if Pluto opposes Saturn, both planets will be involved when the Moon, or one of the personal planets, is in hard aspect to either.

Finally, what are the effects of the planetary aspects? In practice it is the hard aspects from the outer planets – Pluto, Neptune, Uranus, Saturn, Jupiter and Mars – to the Moon, Sun and the inner planets which are relevant. Mars stands between the outer and the inner. It is a personal planet but its aspects to the other personal planets, as well as to the Moon and the Sun, are also potent. The principles of these outer planets, as modifying factors, are as follows.

Pluto — The principle of Pluto is power. The power engendered here is the slow, gradual, deliberate force that rises up from the depths of a volcano, gaining momentum as it pushes its way remorselessly to the surface. The effect is like the build-up of heavy tension with a sense of pressure that threatens to engulf. There is a feeling of being trapped with no way out until the explosion occurs and equilibrium is restored. This power might be used to create a breakthrough where a blockage has arisen but its violence is usually so great that it is difficult to control.

Neptune — Neptune produces a sense of unreality and illusion. There is usually confusion, over-sensitivity, and difficulty in dealing with the material realm. The world becomes a dream; there is often a sense of physical tiredness, with little energy for practical matters. This can lead to loss, delay, deceit. This is therefore a very difficult principle to pin down. If it is balanced with other factors, such as a strong Saturn, it may be used positively in artistic or spiritual ventures, but problems are likely to arise in achieving end results.

Uranus — Uranus is tense, vibrant, exciting, magnetic. The tension of this planet is much more electric than that of Pluto, which is more menacing as it works up from the depths. Uranus, on the other hand, strikes from a clear blue sky with a sudden bolt of lightning. In this way it brings about sudden change and forces a situation to move in a new direction. This energy can be channelled, if care is taken, to produce an individualistic approach that was lacking in the past, although the tyranny of its ways will not be easily tamed.

Saturn — Saturn provides concentration and restriction. Its inhibition can be so great that it kills the life of a venture and we have seen its effects when in hard aspect to the Moon. Frustrations occur because of its slow, deliberate pace and delays are frequent. But it does have great practical power in constructive endeavours and its steadying influence in material affairs should not be underestimated.

Jupiter — Jupiter exaggerates the underlying quality of the time. It is therefore of particular importance to be aware of that quality. All too often it is assumed that expansion can only be positive whereas if Mars is aspecting the Moon in Cancer, and Jupiter's influence is added, the emotional turmoil is merely increased. So bad weather conditions are exacerbated under this planet's influence. On the other hand, expansiveness may be the very quality needed, in which case this energy can be harnessed positively.

Mars — Mars is assertive, aggressive, angry. Its effect is to speed up the quality of the time. There will be a sense of impatience, of anticipation and often a lack of care and consideration for others. Often people will be spoiling for a fight and violence will be likely. If the principle is suitably channelled in a sporting contest, for example, its positive side can be enhanced but care should naturally be taken if it is not to disrupt more peaceful enterprises.

9.

ELECTIONS AND THE NATAL CHART

Vivien Robson states, following Ptolemy: 'Should the nativity or directions indicate failure in any matter, no elections can possibly bring success.'[1] In this chapter I am going to examine the relevance of the natal chart in elections.

As a general statement, the passage I have quoted from Robson shows a total misconception of electional astrology. An electional horoscope represents the time that is right for a particular enterprise. The choice is based on the thesis that every enterprise has its own cycle in time, and choosing the right time means choosing the time that is appropriate for the enterprise rather than for any particular individual.

This point is vital if we are to use elections correctly. Every activity, every principle, every thing has its own life in time just as every human being and every other creature has its life in time. To every thing there is a season and a time to every purpose under the heaven. A city, a ship, a university, a church, each has its own cycle, its moment in time; each rises and falls and rises again according to its own pattern.

This is the starting point. And it is necessary to state this categorically at the outset so that the enterprise and the individual are looked at separately. To say that an election cannot succeed unless it fits in with an individual's horoscope is totally misleading.

That is the general situation. When we come to specific instances, then we must look at each according to its own purpose. Some will depend to a greater or lesser degree on one or more individuals. In some cases, indeed, we will really be dealing with the personal directions of an individual rather than with the principles of elections. Others will stand or fall on their own nature, independent of any person or extraneous organization.

When we ask what relevance a birth chart has to an electional chart we are asking what the coincidence of the two is in any particular instance. In order to appreciate this it is best to view the enterprise and the individual separately at the outset and then ask whether, and if so how, they may coincide in time. We have seen that in approaching an electional chart we choose a particular time on the basis of the time that is most appropriate, according to the cycle of that enterprise and according to the quality of the time which suits that enterprise the best.

We can always separate the enterprise from the individual. Whatever the enterprise may be there will be times which are appropriate and times which are not. So we can choose a time which is right for founding a school or for a marriage according to the cyclic and descriptive principles discussed above.

However, when we move from the general to the particular, we must look at the specific enterprise. Then we must ask: Is it necessary to take into account a natal, or any other, chart when choosing the appropriate time for this enterprise? Whether or not and to what extent it will be necessary to take into account a natal chart will depend entirely on the kind of enterprise under consideration.

Let us take the case of a ship being launched. An enterprise of this kind will not usually be dependent on an individual. Here we are concerned solely with the appropriate time for the ship itself. At the other extreme we can take the case of a baptism. Clearly an enterprise of this kind is a personal one which will depend very much on the individual who is being baptized. Other cases will fall between these two extremes. If a new musical is being launched then not only will the musical itself have its own existence but it may be necessary to consider the position of the producer, the writer, the director and the performers.

Rather than laying down generalized rules, each enterprise should be approached on its own merits. What are we trying to achieve in this particular enterprise? With a musical, are we primarily concerned with the long-term success of the musical itself or are we really interested in the financial prospects of the producer? Whatever the approach we can still see different things by looking at the chart of the enterprise on the one hand and looking at an individual's chart on the other.

The divergence will be apparent if we take an example, which incidentally illustrates the falsity of the statement made by Robson as a general rule, although it may be true in a specific instance. Let us take the example of two people going on a sea journey. In this case the voyage itself may be a success but the situation with regard to the two passengers may be quite different. If we simply look at the natal charts of the two individuals, it may be apparent that one is just not suited to sea travel and is likely to be sick whenever he sets foot on a ship, while the other may be a born sailor. Or, whatever their basic orientation according to their natal charts, if we look at their directions at the time of the voyage, one may be in danger of an accident while the other's directions may be more propitious. The first may fall overboard and drown while the second may fall in love with a fellow passenger.

What then do the charts show? One notorious sea voyage was that of the *Titanic* which sank at 2.20 a.m. on 15 April 1912 after hitting an iceberg the previous evening. The chart for the launch of the ship, at 12.05 p.m. on 31 May 1911, was both the 'birth chart' and the inceptional chart for the launch itself. The chart for its last voyage was at once the horoscope for the voyage itself and also a direction of the original chart. Looking at these two charts, we can see the state of the ship and also the situation with regard to that last, fatal journey.

However, that situation is again quite separate from the situation of any particular passenger or potential passenger. The effects on any one passenger would depend on the coincidence of that passenger's chart with that of the ship. There was no question here of the ship's chart being dependent on an individual. The success of the *Titanic* depended solely on its own chart while the fate of its passengers arose subsequently.

An electional chart therefore shows the time and thereby the quality of the enterprise. How it affects an individual is a matter which depends on the chart of that individual. It has been said that there are good times for kings and good times for cucumbers. There are also good times for religious revival, for poetry, for political parties. And there are good times for individual people who are involved in these activities.

The coincidence of an activity and an individual's success can be seen if we look at the two in specific cases. If we look at an individual poet we see that Jupiter is transiting his Midheaven and we know that this will be a successful time in his career. So his poetry is published. If this is also a good time for poetry in general we may find someone like Lord Byron who woke up one day to find himself famous. But, if it is not, then the personal success fails to break through onto the wider horizons of the world.

Thus when the personal and the mundane cycles coincide the individual personifies his time. It is then that one person is the child, or apotheosis, of his age. Then he or she becomes the focus of that particular time. When the personal and the mundane fail to coincide we get achievements which are great in themselves but, because the time is not then right, do not impinge upon the world until later, if indeed at all. Then the Van Goghs and Gauguins live and die unrecognized until their achievements come to light posthumously.

In magic the paramount importance of the time itself is recognized. From this viewpoint an enterprise is commenced at the time that is right in itself. According to the seasons, the lunar phase, the planetary hours, the right time is chosen depending on the aim of the enterprise. So far as the participants are concerned, it is a question of ensuring that they fit in with the pattern of the time rather than the other way round.

In practice then it is a question of the correct starting point. Should this be the enterprise or the individual? The answer to this question must depend on the specific enterprise.

We can lay down general principles involving different kinds of enterprise. Some will clearly be impersonal while others will be personal. Some will revolve around a number of people, others will be connected to an institution or an organization. But even within the ambit of these general principles each particular enterprise will have its own needs and ultimately it is these which must be taken into account.

If we are looking at an impersonal enterprise, like launching a ship, we should start with the enterprise. The aim of this enterprise is to build a seaworthy ship. The aim of a space launch should similarly be the success of the mission. It is no good trying to arrange the space probe simply to suit one, or even a number, of the participants, and thus threaten the whole programme for the sake of one or more individuals who may not even be fit or alive when the probe is ready for take-off.

Naturally if one particular person is wanted to head the probe, this should be taken into consideration as the chances of success would thereby be enhanced. But as always with elections, the real question is one of choices and of the relative importance of different factors. So far as the starting point is concerned, this must depend on the most important goal of the enterprise.

If the primary aim is the success of the space probe, the starting point must be the launch itself. If it is possible to arrange a coincidence with the astronaut, well and good. But it may not be possible to arrange this, either because the astronaut'a chart is unsuitable in itself, or because it is not the right time for him. In this case it may be that the right choice is to select another astronaut altogether.

On the other hand, when we are dealing with a personal enterprise we will have to take account of the individual's natal chart. So if we want to choose the best time for X to win a race, or set off on a polar expedition, the correct approach is to look first at X's natal chart and then decide on the most appropriate time for him. This will then be primarily a question of looking at his directions and an extension of natal astrology rather than a real case of elections. But even here we can still try to ensure that the day itself is right for the polar expedition or race.

These points illustrate the importance of being quite clear about the goal of the enterprise before choices are made. When we look at a specific venture, we may find it necessary to balance a variety of goals to arrive at an order of priorities. While in most cases it will be obvious whether the enterprise or the individual is to be the starting point, there will be many grey areas in between. The most common involves the setting up of a business where great care must be taken over the role of various individuals.

If a sole practitioner wants to set up a private company, his natal chart must be taken into consideration and will indeed be the starting point. If a partnership decides to turn itself into a limited liability company, the charts of the individual partners will again be of the greatest importance. If a private company is to be floated on the stock exchange, wider considerations must be taken into account.

Naturally in these cases there are likely to be conflicts between the individual natal charts, the charts of the original businesses or companies and the time that would be opportune for the enterprise. It is at this point that the priorities must be appreciated and these will depend on the individual situation alone. If the business is effectively being run by one person, the starting point will have to centre on that person's natal chart. If, on the other hand, there is an optimum time for the enterprise which fits in with the chart of the original business and the other participants, it may be necessary to sacrifice one particular individual.

It may also be pertinent to take account of other charts in a particular case. Thus in a political election the chart of the party, as well as its leader, will be relevant. For a coronation the chart of the nation will be as relevant as that of the ruler. And the coincidence of the mundane and personal charts will also be relevant. To what extent does the leader represent the party and the monarch the nation? The principles are similar to those relating to the individual. There too we need to be sure of the real aim of the enterprise. We shall see the particular relevance of these charts when we look at specific examples of elections in the next chapter.

10.

SPECIFIC ELECTIONS

We have looked at the rules which are applicable in general to electional astrology. We have seen that there are times which in themselves are good as there are times which are bad. So there are times which are right in general for a particular kind of enterprise, while there are others which are inappropriate.

Now we come to specifics. For a particular enterprise the general rules may not be appropriate. Cancer, for example, is the Sign of Mars' fall and therefore in general terms it is not the best place for that planetary energy. Nevertheless, if we want the best day for a swimming contest, this may be the ideal position for Mars.

In this chapter, therefore, I am going to look at some specific elections. Those that I have chosen are not intended to be exhaustive. They represent a selection to illustrate the principles. Nor are the four categories exclusive; they form a natural progression from those enterprises which relate to individuals to those which embrace a wider ambit, but in certain cases they will overlap.

When we look at these examples we should bear in mind that the time we choose symbolizes two separate things. First, it represents the beginning of the enterprise, and it is therefore the horoscope of that enterprise. Second, it reflects the quality of the day or, to be more accurate, of the moment when that enterprise takes place.

The importance of the quality of the day itself will naturally vary according to the nature of the venture. And, to put matters in perspective, in general the less important the enterprise, the more important the quality of the day will be. If, for example, we are choosing the best day for a fun run, a carnival, a horse race, a holiday, or even a marriage, we will want to ensure that the day itself is as auspicious as possible. No one would want to hold a barbecue party in the pouring rain or start their holiday during a thunderstorm. But, even in more important ventures, the quality of the day may be crucial. Setting off on a polar expedition or launching a spaceship in a blizzard would hardly be appropriate.

So far as the electional chart itself is concerned, we should take account of the following. First, we have the solar cycle which represents the time of the year, the seasons of beginning, fruition and culmination and the various crisis periods within the year. Second, there are the planetary cycles which rule the principle or principles of the enterprise. Third, there is the descriptive quality of the time, which is reflected mainly in the Moon's Sign and its aspects. Fourth, we have the mundane sphere as seen in the Angles and the Houses. Here we can see what will occur in detail. In this context we can also arrange for the speed of the inception of the enterprise in the rising Sign, with a Cardinal Sign for action, a Fixed for endurance and a Mutable one for flexibility.

Fifth, we have the lunar phases which correspond on a lesser scale to the solar cycle of the seasons. These relate to giving and receiving, and are of relatively little importance in practice. Of even less importance is the daily cycle from dawn to dusk and back to dawn again which reflects the solar and lunar cycles on a more immediate basis. Sixth, we should be aware of particular problem areas and try to mitigate or balance them if they cannot be avoided. Seventh, we should bear in mind the relevance of other charts. As we saw in the last chapter, these will depend mainly on whether the enterprise is personal or impersonal.

When we set about the task of selecting the best time for our enterprise, we should take account of these points. It is not of course a question of simply taking them in order. As a matter of convenience I have listed them in an approximate order of importance, but in practice they must be synthesized. In any particular enterprise one point may be of greater importance than another and we must in all cases look at the specific enterprise and make the necessary choices accordingly. I shall now look at some examples to illustrate these points and as well as stating the general principles I shall use some inceptional Charts to show how the principles relate to particular ventures.

Elections for individuals and couples

Because these are enterprises that concern just one or two people it will be necessary to take account of the birth charts of the individuals concerned. Choosing the right time for a baptism, for example, will mean looking at the baby's natal chart to begin with, and this will be even more pertinent when we are dealing with medical operations.

Nevertheless, the day itself will still be relevant. There are times which are in themselves good for travel or moving house just as there are days which are difficult for a particular kind of operation. Similarly, when we look at an individual's natal chart it may be apparent that he should not embark on a particular kind of enterprise at all, or at least not without great care. We may be deciding on an auspicious day for an individual to initiate litigation but when we look at his birth chart we find that he would be well advised to avoid the courts altogether. Naturally in the examples I am taking here we can only look at the electional principles although in an actual case the birth chart may take precedence.

Elections for individuals

Baptism — As a church service this comes under the general rulership of Jupiter. The quality of the day should be calm and peaceful, especially if a long Catholic service is being performed and the baby is no longer young. The 5th House, ruling children, should be taken into account, and hard aspects from Uranus and Mars avoided. For the baptism of our six-month old daughter I chose a day when the Moon was in Libra, which coincided with her Sun and rising sign. During the half-hour service she was perfectly quiet and happy, much to the suprise of the priest and in marked contrast to her usual behaviour, and the party held afterwards was equally harmonious.

Travel — Travel in general comes under the rulership of Mercury. The purpose of the travel will naturally vary depending on whether it is a holiday or a business trip. The traditional distinction between 'long' and 'short' journeys is no longer valid and therefore Jupiter has no relevance here. In addition to Mercury's position, the early parts of the Sun's and the Moon's cycles are most appropriate.

As we are concerned with the beginnings and movement, the rising Sign will be important. Here Cardinal Signs will be most appropriate, the Sign itself correlating with the kind of travel. So Libra would be best for air travel, Cancer for sea voyages and Capricorn for travel by land. However, if speed is the main requirement, then Aries should take precedence over a slower Sign like Capricorn or Cancer.

The 3rd and 9th Houses should be taken into account, especially to ensure that no difficult factors are placed there. Finally, the quality of the journey and the subsequent period will be reflected in the position of the Moon. This body's position in Sagittarius would get a holiday off to a bright, adventurous start, while the Moon's position in Pisces square Mars would provide a stormy sea passage and an emotionally exhausting trip.

Moving house — Here we shall be concerned with the quality of the day rather than the house. The Moon as well as Mercury will therefore be important in this case. In so far as a journey is being undertaken, the same points will apply as to travel in general.

Careers — Starting a new job, Mercury, Venus and Mars should be taken into account. Points to avoid are hard aspects from Neptune, which would induce confusion or fraud, and from Pluto, which are likely to introduce power conflicts. For detailed, conscientious work, Virgo and Capricorn should be stressed. Finally, it is important to bear in mind the type of work involved. Capricorn is appropriate for work in general, but Leo would be more suitable for a theatrical career while Scorpio would be better for scientific research or pathology.

Financial affairs — These include investments, buying and selling shares, buying property or land. The purpose of these enterprises must be clear at the outset, especially whether they are speculation, investment or buying property in order to live in it. Mercury rules commerce in the sense of buying and selling, Venus rules money, Saturn long-term investments and Jupiter the solid benefits that accrue. For buying property the Moon is also important, especially if it is to be a home. When looking at the aspects, Jupiter is relevant for gains and Saturn for steady investments.

If the transaction is buying a home, then the 4th House is extremely important. Any planets in this House, especially those near the IC will show specific problems or benefits depending on the planet and its aspects. Neptune in difficult aspect, for example, would suggest trouble with the drains.

Legal matters — Mercury governs day-to-day affairs concerning litigation, signing contracts and general legal procedure. The main consideration here is to ensure that problem aspects to Mercury are avoided: Neptune with regard to fraud or confusion, Saturn in respect of delays and frustration and Jupiter for over-optimism and errors of judgement. In litigious situations the 7th House relates to the other party in the case.

Medical operations — This is a very specialized subject and great care should be taken when dealing with medical matters. Clearly the natal chart of the patient will be of the greatest importance in this type of case. But in many cases there will be very little time available to make a choice and the quality of the time itself should never be underestimated. There are days when the risk of accidents is high and hospital staff have noted definite patterns ranging from periods when they are filled to capacity with emergencies which contrast with others when they are almost unnaturally quiet.

Similarly, there are times when the body bleeds more profusely than others and these days were recognized even in Anglo-Saxon times as we saw in Chapter 3. So far as human anatomy is concerned the parts of the body are ruled by the Signs and not, as some texts state, by the planets which rule those Signs. Mars rules the operation itself, while the Moon reflects the quality of the day. Here the situation needs to be seen in context. We would hardly expect a pleasant day for an unpleasant operation but a time which specifically suggests danger to the area in question should be avoided. So if Mars is square a conjunction of the Moon and Neptune is in Pisces there will be excessive bleeding, and if the Moon also makes a hard aspect to Jupiter the situation will be exacerbated.

Elections for couples — Here again the natal charts will be important, not only in themselves but so far as mutual compatibility is concerned. This indeed will be the primary consideration for any joint venture. The starting point will therefore be the natal charts of the persons concerned. We can choose an appropriate time for a joint venture by looking at the directions of the individuals and also by looking at the quality of the time from the point of view of elections. But if the natal charts are not compatible to start with then no long-term success will ensue.

Marriage and engagement — Having taken into account the natal charts and the directions from these, we should try to provide a day which will both ensure a happy relationship and which will be congenial in itself. Venus will rule the relationship, Mars the physical compatibility, the 7th House the way the parties view each other, the 4th House the domestic environment, the 5th House the children, and the 2nd and 8th Houses the emotional and physical needs which the parties can share. To ensure an agreeable day for the ceremony itself, the Moon's position should be given priority.

Here too there will be a need for balance. Expansion and hope will be needed from Jupiter but Saturn's influence should also provide responsibility and protection if the marriage is to endure. Similarly, a mixture of Cardinal and Fixed Signs will ensure that there is activity and endurance without too much rigidity or impatience. We can look at two well-known royal marriages to see the situation in those cases.

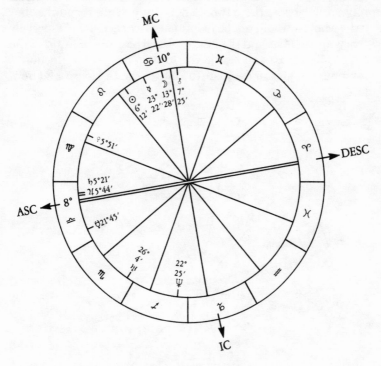

Figure 10.1 Horoscope for the wedding of Prince Charles and Lady Diana Spencer
11.17 a.m. BST, 29 July 1981, London (51N30, 0W07)

The first is that of Prince Charles and Lady Diana Spencer whose wedding chart is illustrated in Fig. 10.1. Venus is rather weak here, being in the Sign of its fall and hardly aspected. However, it makes no hard aspects which is a positive point in practice and it makes a sextile aspect to Mars which is also beneficial. The Moon's position in Cancer being close to the Midheaven is in itself positive and it is compatible with Lady Diana's natal chart which has her Sun in that Sign. So far as aspects to the Moon are concerned, the situation is not so promising with a conjunction to Mars and a wide square to the Jupiter–Saturn conjunction as well as to Pluto, with the Moon near the mid-point of those planets. However, the aspects are all separating except the one to Pluto.

Libra as the rising Sign is favourable for a marriage although the Saturn–Jupiter conjunction so close to the Ascendant could be a problem. In theory these two planets can balance each other but on the whole it would not be helpful to place them here, especially as they square Mars and the Midheaven. The Sun's position in the 10th House in Leo and sextile the Jupiter–Saturn conjunction is propitious but Mercury's square to Pluto in the 1st House is far from ideal.

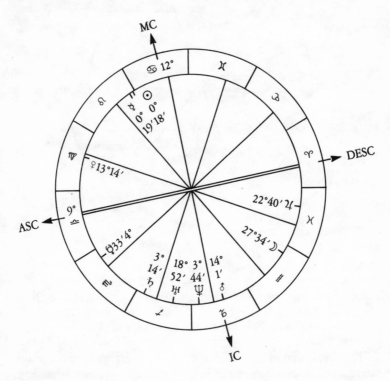

Figure 10.2 Horoscope for the wedding of Prince Andrew and Sarah Ferguson 11.50 a.m. BST, 23 July 1986, Westminster, London (51N30, 0W07)

The wedding chart of Prince Andrew and Sarah Ferguson has the Angles in almost the same position as that of the Prince and Princess of Wales. Once again Venus is in Virgo, this time applying to a square aspect with Uranus, which could be very difficult. The Moon is applying to a square aspect with Saturn which, as we saw in the charts of well-known disasters, is hardly helpful. The Sun and Mercury are also applying to a square with Pluto. There are no favourable planets near the Angles to strengthen the chart and Mars close to the IC is again a difficult indication. On the whole this chart, illustrated in Fig. 10.2, is far from ideal.

Business partnerships — Here too it is essential to start with and to ensure the compatibility of the respective natal charts. It will also be necessary not only to arrange a good time for the business venture in general with Mercury and Venus well placed but also to take account of the particular kind of business. An art gallery would come under Venus, and Libra should be emphasized. A shop would be governed by Mercury, a comedy team would be helped by the humour and versatility of Leo and Gemini, and a skating partnership would be assisted by the qualities of physical co-ordination, timing, muscular strength — a combination of Venus, Mercury and Mars.

Elections for groups

An electional chart for a group will be more impersonal than one for an individual or couple. Here the emphasis will be on the enterprise itself rather than on the participators.

Social gatherings and parties — The most important considerations for these events will be the quality of the day. Therefore the position of the Moon will be paramount. Leo, or alternatively Libra, will be the best Sign for that body. If the event is to take place outside, weather conditions should be taken into account. A Fire Sign would be best to ensure sunshine, followed by an Air Sign, the latter also helping with communication and conversation. Water Signs would not be appropriate, providing rain and too much emotion, while the Earth Signs would be dull.

Charity events — These would include sponsored events, for example a walk or swim or fun run. Once again the quality of the day will be important but here we can differentiate rather more, depending on the kind of event. From the spectators' point of view, the weather should preferably be dry for a fun run or walk though it should not be too hot for the participants. For a carnival the weather will be of even greater importance. For a swimming event the Moon should be in a Water Sign.

For a race, Mars should be in evidence, preferably rising. This is a good example of the particular taking precedence over the general. As we have seen, planets close to the Angles are powerful and in practice they are likely to produce problems. But in appropriate cases they can be used positively, although even then it is necessary to appreciate the potential dangers. Jupiter either rising or in hard aspect to the Moon would provide a sense of expansiveness and buoyancy.

Sports contests — The difference between these events and the previous ones lies in their adversarial nature. In a charity event, although there is a race, the main importance lies in the event itself and in raising money for the charity. In a contest, on the other hand, the main interest will be in the winner, although a secondary consideration may be the quality of the day, especially if it is regarded as a day out.

If, as is likely, the main consideration lies in choosing the winner of the contest, there will be comparatively little scope for the principles of electional astrology. Here the starting point will be the birth charts of the individual contestants. In a boxing match, for example, these can be compared directly and the directions of each taken into account for the date of the match. To a limited extent we can decide from the individual natal charts the kind of day that would suit any particular contestant the best. For example, in a horse race, one horse may perform better in heavy going than another.

Forming a club — As an activity which involves sharing and acting in concert this comes under the rulership of Venus which should be given priority. Mercury will also be important for communicating between members. The Moon would be placed most appropriately in one of the Air Signs to aid the exchange of ideas although the kind of club should be taken into account. There should also be some emphasis on the Earth Signs to ensure that the practicalities are taken care of.

In the diurnal cycle we should pay attention to the 11th House which is always important in group activities and especially in clubs. It may be possible to place the Moon, Venus, Mercury or the Sun here. But they should only be placed in this House if they make no difficult aspects, otherwise any problems that exist will be exaggerated.

Commercial enterprises and mergers of firms and companies — Commercial activities in general come under the rulership of Mercury which should be placed in an appropriate Sign. We should also ensure that no difficult aspects are made to this planet. Venus will be important both with regard to the financial side and also for the harmony necessary for a successful merger. If these are to be profitable in the long term, it would be advisable to have a Fixed Sign on the Ascendant: Taurus for straightforward commercial success, Scorpio for shared interests, Aquarius where people and ideas are stressed and Leo where one party is taking over another.

For long-term prosperity the area around the Midheaven, including the 9th and 10th Houses, should also be emphasized, preferably with the Sun or Moon in that part of the diurnal cycle. Emphasis should additionally be placed on the Earth Signs, especially Capricorn and Taurus for practical endeavour, while Libra and Aquarius would be appropriate for sharing on a personal level.

Although a merger is a commercial enterprise, it is analogous to a marriage on a personal level. What we are concerned with here is the compatibility of two entities. Naturally commercial considerations will take precedence, but it will still be necessary to ensure that the two entities function together. Certainly if the charts of the organizations themselves are incompatible then there will be no success for a merger in the long term although it may be possible in a particular case to dissolve a company and form a completely new organization. So far as a firm is concerned, as we are dealing with a partnership the natal charts of the partners must also be taken into account.

For a new partnership, whether in the strict sense of a merged firm or the consolidation of two companies, the 7th House will be crucial. This area could contain Venus, Mercury, the Sun or the Moon, provided no difficult aspects are made to these bodies. It is essential that this House does not contain problem planets or any planets in difficult aspect.

Branch offices — These too, as commercial enterprises, come under the general rulership of Mercury. As the offspring of the parent company, the 5th House will be emphasized and the 6th will be of subsidiary importance with regard to day-to-day work. It is important that the chart of the parent company is taken into account to ensure that the two are compatible and especially that there are no problem areas from the 4th or 10th House or between the Sun or Moon.

Agriculture, farming and gardening — Many of the old astrology texts are replete with agricultural and gardening lore. This is hardly surprising given the importance of agriculture and the involvement of a large part of the population in that industry. Even today those concerned with the land are often closer to nature and its rhythms than the rest of the population.

Farming today can of course be as much a commercial enterprise as the production of motor vehicles. Nevertheless it will inevitably be geared to the solar cycle we examined in a previous chapter, even if this is sometimes taken for granted or even surperseded by artificial methods. Planting and reaping are also one of the main exceptions regarding the importance of the lunar phases.

We have seen that in general the importance of the Moon lies in its Signs and aspects. Contrary to the statements in old books of astrology, the phases of the Moon are for the most part relatively unimportant. In general they follow the analogy of the solar cycle with the waxing phase being most appropriate for beginning an enterprise and the waning phase for completing it. But on the physical level the magnetic attraction so readily seen in the tides also affects the earth and thus the best time for sowing is after the New Moon while the best time for reaping, as well as destroying weeds and felling trees, is from the last quarter to the New Moon.

Elections for organizations

Our horizons widen further as we look at the foundation of institutions of various kinds: places of learning, religion, the law, hospitals, prisons, entertainment, commercial ventures and also the launching of ships, aircraft, rockets and space probes.

Places of learning — Universities, polytechnics, colleges and schools. All learning comes under the rulership of Mercury, which governs the principle of communication. However, the purpose of communication, the goal of learning, differs. And in looking at these goals we can see the reason for Mercury ruling two very different Signs. Superficially there is little in common between Gemini and Virgo, except that they are both Mutable Signs.

Gemini, as an Air Sign, is concerned with communication betweem human beings, with words, speech and the exchange of ideas. Virgo, as an Earth Sign, is concerned primarily with craftsmanship, and with learning practical skills and techniques. It is this which creates the tangible basis of any art form, including writing which is fashioned from the Geminian word.

It is therefore necessary first to decide the kind of learning that forms the goal of the enterprise, and second, the specific quality that is required for the venture. While in certain cases these two points may coincide, the principles are separate and are based on the two kinds of time I have discussed, the cyclic and descriptive respectively. The first step consists in choosing the Sign most appropriate for Mercury as the ruler of the enterprise, which would normally be Gemini or Virgo.

This point is of practical importance because Mercury has its detriment in Sagittarius and its fall in Pisces and yet both these Signs are appropriate for different kinds of learning, especially the former with its association with higher learning and philosophy. We can then go on to the next step and place the Moon in the Sign that describes the desired quality of the particular institution.

If a university is being established, Mercury should be placed in Gemini for the primary goal is intellectual learning. For a polytechnic, with the emphasis more on practical endeavour, Virgo should be selected. At this stage only do we come to the specific quality of the institution. Here it is the Moon's Sign that takes precedence. For a place of higher learning, Sagittarius would be appropriate; we might choose Aquarius if the emphasis were on research, Cancer for an infant school to bring out the qualities of caring and protectiveness, Libra for an art school, Leo for drama and so on.

The diurnal cycle, focused on the Ascendant, is concerned with the endurance of the establishment. It might be assumed that a Mutable Sign at this point would be appropriate but this would be a mistake. The flexibility of the enterprise should be contained primarily in the position of the ruling planet and secondly in the quality of the enterprise as reflected in the Moon's position. The diurnal cycle is concerned with the manifestation of the enterprise in mundane terms, with its inception and with how it will develop in day-to-day terms. If the institution is to survive, then on no account should a Mutable Sign be placed on the Ascendant.

Places of religious worship — The ruling planet for churches and other places of worship is Jupiter, with Neptune as a subsidiary ruler in accordance with the latter's role as a spiritual energy. Naturally, in view of the time Neptune takes to move round the Zodiac, there will be no question of choosing its Sign, and even with Jupiter there may be comparatively little choice. Saturn, as the planet of social order, and Venus, signifying harmony and love, are also relevant.

Here, as in all cases, we must first establish a priority of aims. Is it to be the spiritual quality of the enterprise, the social well-being

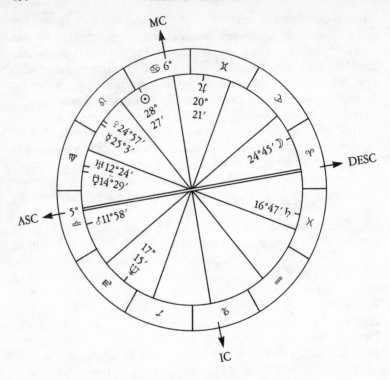

Figure 10.3 Horoscope for St Gregory's church
11.30 a.m. BST, 21 July 1965, Eastbourne, Sussex (50N46, 0E18)

of the community, the building itself of some other goal? The answer
to these questions will determine the choice of the Moon's position,
whether this should be in a caring Sign like Pisces or Cancer or in
a more practical Sign like Capricorn or Taurus, for example.

At this point we can look at the chart of the foundation of a Roman
Catholic church known to the author, which is illustrated in Figure
10.3. The time for the church was not elected but it is of interest
in seeing the problems that can arise as well as the more positive
indications. The ruler, Jupiter, is in Gemini, the Sign of its detriment.
It is elevated in the 9th House which is a reasonably strong position
in this particular context but it forms a T-square with Uranus and
Pluto on one side and Saturn on the other.

The Moon's position in the aggressive Sign of Aries has not been
conducive to the well-being of either the parish or the structure of
the church. The majority of its priests have aroused hostility among
their parishioners, one of them being forced to leave because of his

relationship with a female member of the parish and another being quietly retired to the country. However, there are no difficult aspects to the Moon except a square to the Sun, and it makes a close applying trine to Venus and Mercury. Other incumbents have succeeded in restoring a sense of community and enterprise, though not without some controversy among the more traditional residents.

The most serious problem has related to the physical structure of the building with the fear that the church may have to be pulled down and the consequent threat of litigation with the architect and builders. Certainly Mars rising in Libra bodes ill on the material level as it does on the personal, while Neptune in the 2nd House (which relates to the physical construction), applying to a square with Venus and Mercury, is hardly helpful.

Legal establishments — Law courts, legal centres. Legal matters come under the aegis of Jupiter. If we are concerned with a law court as a building, Capricorn should be emphasized and a Fixed Sign should rise, preferably Taurus. Planets close to the Ascendant should be avoided if possible, and otherwise noted with great care. Libra, as the principle of justice, should also be emphasized if possible.

If we are involved in a legal advice centre, then we shall be more concerned with communicating and caring and we should look at Mercury and, to a lesser extent, Venus. Cancer and Pisces would provide the requisite human quality, while Libra would again reflect the principle of justice as well as the one-to-one advice itself.

Hospitals and prisons — Mental asylums as well as general hospitals, rehabilitation centres and hostels may be included under the general heading of incarceration. The 12th House will be important in the diurnal cycle and we should ensure that this area is free from difficult planets or planets making difficult aspects.

The ruling planets are Saturn and Neptune but as their motion is so slow it is unlikely that there will be any choice with regard to their Signs. Venus will also be relevant for hospitals and Mercury for mental institutions. In the latter case Pisces may be an appropriate position even though it is the Sign of its fall and detriment.

The emphasis of particular qualities will naturally vary although the same basic thread runs through all these establishments. Caring will always be an issue of importance, more so in hospitals, mental institutions and rehabilitation centres than in prisons where security will assume a greater role. Security too will have its relevance in rehabilitation centres and to a lesser degree in psychiatric establishments.

For a caring quality, Pisces or Cancer would be appropriate; for a more paternalistic ethos, Capricorn would be apt. For security we would look to Saturn and ensure that Neptune did not make hard aspects to important factors in the chart, especially to the Moon, the Angles or any ruling planets.

Entertainment and leisure — Theatres, the cinema, concert halls, opera and other musical events, hotels, restaurants, conference centres, leisure centres, sports centres, swimming pools and marinas can all be classified under this heading. Venus rules pleasure in general and the arts in particular. Mars rules enterprises of a more combative nature. Mercury will be more relevant for a conference centre.

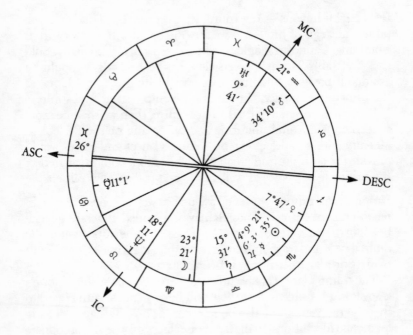

Figure 10.4 Horoscope for the first broadcast of the BBC
6 p.m. GMT, 14 November 1922, London (51N31, 0W06)

For general enjoyment, Leo and Libra would be appropriate Signs for the Moon, but for more outgoing forms of entertainment Sagittarius and Aries would be better, while for sailing or swimming the Moon should be placed in a Water Sign, preferably Cancer or

Pisces. Taurus would be suitable for the opera and Pisces for the ballet. The particular kind of entertainment would also determine the Ascending Sign. For a sports centre, a Cardinal Sign should be chosen, Aries for energetic, competitive games like squash, Cancer for water sports. For a hotel or restaurant, a Fixed Sign like Taurus or Leo would be more appropriate, while Aquarius would be right for a conference centre.

Commercial operations — The stock market, publishing and the media, building bridges and tunnels. We have looked at some commercial operations in the last section and noted that in general they fall under the rulership of Mercury. The financial side of commerce is more particularly governed by Venus although in some ventures like the stock market Saturn will also be relevant. Publishing and the media come under Mercury, and the Air Signs in general should be emphasized, Gemini for newspapers and magazines and the radio, and Aquarius and Libra for television.

We can see in Fig. 10.4 the chart set up for the first broadcast of the BBC which appropriately has Gemini rising. It is a strong chart with some controversy reflected in the elevated Mars in Aquarius making a square aspect to the Mercury–Jupiter conjunction in Scorpio. Uranus is the most elevated planet which is symbolic of this venture and it forms the apex of a Grand Trine with the Mercury–Jupiter conjunction just mentioned and Pluto in the 1st House. The Moon is in the practical Sign of Virgo in the 3rd House of communications and makes no difficult aspect.

Bridges and tunnels also come directly under the rulership of Mercury. Here, with construction emphasized, Saturn will also be important and naturally stability will be of the utmost importance. Therefore Taurus, Capricorn and the Fixed Signs generally should be in evidence. For determination and strength of purpose, Mars' position should be taken into account.

Launching ships, aircraft and rockets — With the emphasis on travel, Mercury will be the planet governing these enterprises. Uranus will be relevant in space travel and Mars in military missions. Jupiter as the expansive principle wil also hold a subsidiary role. These are active enterprises and therefore Mars will also be relevant in general terms. For the same reason speed and thrust will be emphasized and a Cardinal Sign rising will normally be appropriate.

The diurnal cycle will indeed be of particular importance in these operations because the quality of the day, and the moment of inception, will determine their ultimate success to a very great degree. Here the end will be reflected in the beginning in a way which lays peculiar emphasis on the initial circumstances surrounding the enterprise.

If a space probe is to be launched on a freezing day the venture will be doomed from the start, as the *Challenger* disaster showed. It is therefore vital to ensure that the Angles and Houses reflect this emphasis. Sagittarius, Aries or Cancer for a ship and Gemini for an aircraft would be suitable rising Signs. The proximity of any planet to the Ascendant and to a lesser extent to the other Angles should be noted with the greatest care. The speed of the beginning, and therefore of the enterprise as a whole, will be reflected especially in the rising Sign and to a lesser extent in the Moon's Sign.

We can see illustrated in Fig. 10.5 the launching of a well-known ship, the *Titanic*, on 31 May 1911. Here the Moon's position is especially unfortunate. Although the conjunction with Neptune is

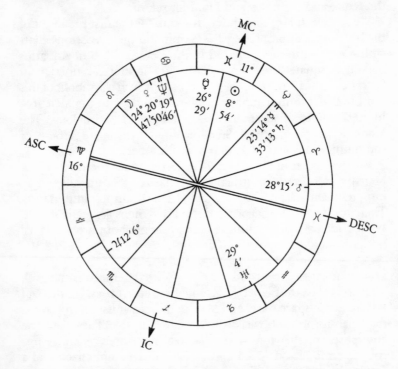

Figure 10.5 Horoscope for the launching of the *Titanic*
12.05 p.m. LT, 31 May 1911, Belfast (54N36, 5W57)

separating, it is applying to an opposition with Uranus. In addition there is a close conjunction between Mercury and Saturn in Taurus in the 8th House and Mars in Pisces makes a close square aspect to an elevated Pluto. The weakness of Virgo as a rising Sign is also apparent as it is in many charts that fail to provide an enterprise with sufficient endurance or resilience.

National and international elections
In ancient times it was for the foundation of a new city or state that electional astrology was almost exclusively used. Whether these choices have been successful only history can tell. In this section I shall look at the principles upon which these wider-reaching enterprises may be based.

Nations and states — The principle of government comes under the Sun, while the establishment of the government itself falls within

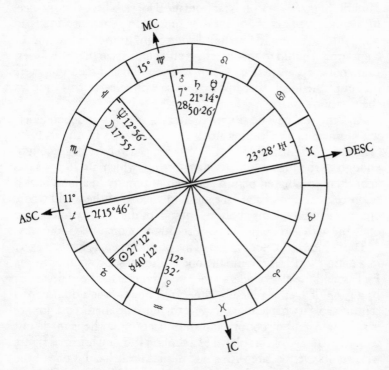

Figure 10.6 Horoscope for Burma
4.20 a.m. LT, 4 January 1948, Rangoon (16N45, 96E20)

the ambit of Jupiter. The Moon should be placed in a stable position, preferably in one of the Cardinal or Fixed Signs and the Ascendant should also be in a Sign which emphasizes permanence. Mutable Signs should therefore be avoided. The best balance would be to have the Moon in a Fixed Sign such as Leo and the Ascendant in a Cardinal Sign like Libra or Capricorn.

It is in these mundane charts that the diurnal cycle is of particular importance. Here the dangers and potentials can clearly be seen in the various areas of a country's existence. Few nations have chosen their own times of birth but such a one was Burma whose electional chart is illustrated in Fig. 10.6. This chart is a good example both of the consequences of failing to take into account certain factors and of misinterpreting others.

In this electional chart, Jupiter rises in Sagittarius and presumably it was for that reason that the chart was chosen, although it meant that the annual festivities take place at 4.20 a.m. each year. As a Mutable Sign, Sagittarius is far from ideal for stability or endurance. In theory it represents openness, wisdom and generosity and is an outgoing, positive and freedom-loving Sign. Jupiter, as the ruler of Sagittarius, should in theory reflect and emphasize these qualities. Faith, hope, expansiveness, wealth, co-operation and friendship were no doubt the ideals that inspired those who selected this time for their nation's birth.

And the result? The situation after 40 years of 'independence' was summed up in a leading article in *The Times* on 12 August 1988: 'The long-suffering people of Burma appear to have had enough; enough of the brutal military dictatorship, which for 26 years has kept them in isolated penury; enough of poverty in a land of rich resources; enough of state socialism in an area of the world where entrepreneurial talents abound; enough of the security forces who open fire with automatic weapons on crowds of unarmed protestors.'

The sadness is that today most of the Burmese people live in poverty in a nation which is potentially one of the most prosperous in the Far East and the independence they were granted has been destroyed by a gang of ageing generals who seized power over a quarter of a century ago. So what lessons can we learn from this chart? First, Jupiter is not the herald of bounty and munificence that he is made out to be. The image of this planet as a smiling Father Christmas figure who grants every desire with a nod of his kindly head is one of the most damaging in astrology. Hope there may be but as often hope unfulfilled; expansion too but in what direction and for whose benefit?

Furthermore, by having Jupiter conjunct the Ascendant, Mars was automatically placed on the Midheaven which led to the brutal regime of the generals. All things are connected. When we place one factor in a chart we must look at the result in terms of the other factors that are thereby displaced.

The other major drawback in this chart was that no account was taken of Neptune. The failure to take this outer planet into consideration is clear when we note its position in the chart. Without Neptune the Moon, so important in electional charts, is well placed. It is in Libra which is appropriate enough for a state, with the emphasis on justice and order, and it makes no difficult aspects to other planets apart from the separating square to the Sun and Mercury. But Neptune is at 12 degrees 56 minutes of Libra and is thus not only conjunct the Moon but makes an exact square aspect to both the Sun and Mercury. Small wonder then that the people of this nation have been cheated by their leaders.

Some countries have had more success than others with their beginnings. In May 1988 Woodrow Wyatt wrote an account of how he accompanied Sir Stafford Cripps on the Cabinet mission to India in 1947 in order to arrange independence for that country and Pakistan.[1] The Cabinet had chosen 14 August as the date for independence and, while Jinnah of the Muslim League was happy to accept that day, the Indian leaders were troubled.

The advice of the Indian astrologers was that 14 August was an inauspicious day. However, they could only try to mitigate the situation by choosing the best, or at any rate the least inappropriate, time during that day. They came up with midnight. As Wyatt wrote: 'So Pakistan began its independence in the morning and India in the middle of the night. India's subsequent history has been somewhat more successful than Pakistan's.'

There will often be the temptation to try to arrange a nation's chart around that of its leader. While this may be advantageous for the leader in question, it could have very deleterious results in the long term. A nation will continue to exist after any one of its leaders has died and to fetter its future to the past in this way can only restrict its natural development.

Coronations — Here we have the opposite situation and clearly the time for a coronation should fit in with both the charts of the monarch and of the state. As a regal event Leo should be emphasized, preferably with the Moon in that Sign. Endurance and stability should be the qualities stressed by the rising Sign. The 10th House as the outward aspirations of the nation and the 4th as the foundations of the State are of especial importance.

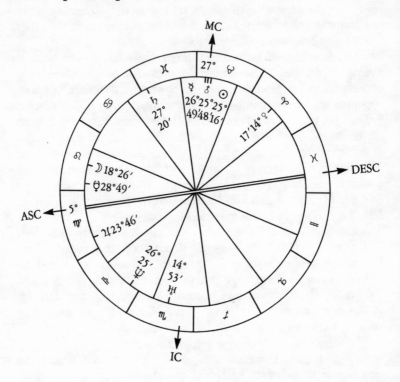

Figure 10.7 Horoscope for the coronation of King Edgar
Noon LMT, 11 May 973 (OS), Bath (51N22, 2W22)

I have illustrated the coronation of King Edgar in 973 here in Fig. 10.7. This took place not at the beginning of Edgar's reign but to consolidate his position as leader of England's rulers. The Midheaven is clearly emphasized with the Sun, Mars and Mercury conjunct that point. The Moon is in an appropriate Sign in Leo but its position in the 12th House is weak and it squares Uranus on one side and the conjunction of the Sun, Mars and Mercury on the other. Virgo rising is also not an ideal Ascendant.

New cities and towns — Electional charts for the foundation of cities were common in the early days of astrology although unfortunately many principles were not appreciated in those times and the outer planes were as yet undiscovered. The rules relating to the cities and town are similar to those for states but on a smaller scale. Indeed it is only the scale that differs. In principle there is no distinction between a state and a city as is apparent when we consider the Greek city-states.

However, as a matter of emphasis, the Sun will not be so important, while the Moon, representing the people, will assume greater significance. Mercury, governing communications, will also be of greater relevance. The diurnal cycle will again show the areas of importance in the life of the community and any areas of danger which should be avoided.

Agreements and treaties — These embrace a wide variety of events, from summits between the superpowers discussing peace and nuclear disarmament, trade agreements between nations, treaties forging links in various areas, in the economic sphere, for example, as with the EEC, or with more specialized goals, to control marine pollution or to restrict fishing rights.

As the aim of any agreement is to reach an accomodation, the placing of Venus will be of great importance. Mercury, representing the actual process of communication, will also be relevant. The position of Mars should be taken into account to avoid disruptions and disputes.

In general the diurnal cycle will show the areas of special importance where problems may arise. The 7th House relates to the process of agreement, while the 10th House shows how the parties will attempt to project their endeavours. The 9th House will relate to their visions and ideals and the 3rd to the discussions themselves. The Moon should be in a Cardinal Sign. Mutable Signs will produce interminable negotiations which are unlikely to be resolved, while the Fixed Signs will lead to stalemate.

A Fixed Sign rising should also be avoided if possible. Here a Mutable Sign would be best, providing flexibility and the ability to manoeuvre, although Virgo could be too critical and Pisces could lead to confusion. When we come to the particular kind of treaty we can pay closer attention to the details of the chart. A nuclear disarmament or non-proliferation treaty should emphasize peace with Libra being prominent and no stressful aspects from Mars,. Uranus or Pluto. An agreement relating to fishing rights would naturally emphasize the Water Signs; in a commercial treaty, Mercury and the Earth Signs would be prominent.

Political parties — Much will depend on the kind of party, whether Conservative, Socialist, Green or whatever. Two general principles, however, should be born in mind. First, the aim of any party will be to win power. Therefore the chart should be one which involves acceptance and confidence from the voters. Second, it should propagate its particular aims. Also, as the party will ultimately represent the state when in power, there should be positive links between it and the national chart.

In order to gain credence, the people's confidence and respect is necessary and here the Moon will be emphasized. The type of acceptance depends on the kind of party we are dealing with. One that appeals to a conservative element will emphasize traditional Signs like Capricorn or Leo. One that appeals more to the people will have the Moon in Aquarius or Cancer. An ecologically based party could have the Moon placed in Virgo, and one appealing to a religious cause would have that body more appropriately placed in Pisces.

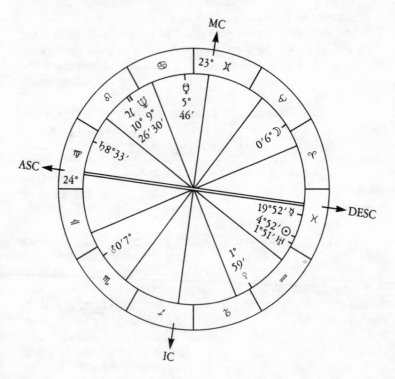

Figure 10.8 Horoscope for the foundation of the Nazi party
7.29 p.m. LT, 24 February 1920, Munich, Germany (48N08, 11E34)

In terms of leadership the Sun is important. From the point of view of communicating to the voters, Mercury should be taken into account, while the establishment of the body of the party will be ruled by Jupiter. The 10th House shows the image projected by the party to the world at large, the 4th its foundations. The 11th is also important in attracting groups.

A chart for the foundation of the Nazi party is given here in Fig. 10.8. With Pluto elevated in the 10th House the emphasis is on power, and with the 4th House empty the foundations are weak. Virgo rising may appeal to the working classes and the people in general in the short term, but with Mercury in Pisces unaspected in the 6th House, the ability to communicate its message on a wider basis is severely circumscribed.

The chart is in fact an interesting mixture of a vision of power being imposed on a deeply troubled substratum. The position of Pluto in the 10th mentioned above is enforced by its being at the apex of a Grand Trine linking Mars and the Sun–Uranus conjunction. However, Mars also forms part of a Grand Cross embracing the Moon in Taurus, the Jupiter–Neptune conjunction in the 11th and Venus in Aquarius. The Fixed Signs of this latter configuration emphasize the terrible power that the party wielded over the nation which proved so self-destructive in the long term.

Political elections — In one sense the choice of timing for a political election falls into a class of its own. In a general election the result means success or failure for the party and the leader whose decision it was to call the election. There is no middle way. In the case of Edward Heath, whom I shall use to illustrate this kind of election, the effects of bad timing were even more profound for they led to his personal downfall from which he never recovered.

In another sense too a political election differs from other types of elections, for in this case there is an adversarial situation. A choice must be made to secure victory. But victory for one party inevitably means defeat for another. Therefore it is not just a question of choosing the right time objectively, but specifically the right time for the party, and to an extent the leader of that party which is calling the election.

Before we look at the chart of one particular election, let us examine in more detail the points at issue. What is it we want to achieve in selecting a date for a general election? Obviously the aim is to win the election. The crucial question is therefore: 'Will *I* win the election?' rather than: 'What kind of election will this be?'

On the face of it, it may appear that we are therefore only concerned with arranging a day that will be compatible with the party and its leader. But we can go much further than this. Certain conditions will suit certain parties and certain conditions will be more favourable for the party in power than for those in opposition. Such is the art of timing whose lessons need to be learned.

One of the major problems that has faced the Labour party in this country is that the more prosperous the nation the less its chances have been of gaining power, and the more prosperous its supporters have become the less inclined they have been to support their party. Certainly a booming economy is likely to help the Conservatives while industrial unrest will be likely to favour the Socialists. Even in these circumstances, however, timing is vital, for the pendulum can swing very quickly in political life. As Harold Wilson once said: 'In politics, a week is a long time.'

A time of industrial unrest may bring out the socialist votes but if the demands of the unions become too strident a reaction can set in as Mrs Thatcher found to her advantage with the coal miners. Often the worst enemy of a party is apathy, brought about by disinterest or even bad weather or the holiday season. The time of year, or the solar cycle, is important in this respect. Winter is a time of discontent which favours opposition, summer is a time of calm and ease which favours the party in power, and spring heralds a new start where there is more life and inducement to bring people to the poll.

The question will therefore be: 'What kind of day will ensure that the supporters of the party calling the election will turn out to vote?' That the art of timing is inherent in a politician's success is something accepted instinctively by those involved in government. Such a one was Clement Attlee who, when asked why he had resigned the party leadership in December 1955, replied. 'One has to watch times and seasons, you know.'[2]

That the subtle art of timing is often as unobtrusive as the inflexions of a good actor was recognized by Tom Jones, secretary to the Cabinet when Stanley Baldwin called the general election for 14 November 1935, gaining a majority of 247 over the combined opposition. Jones remarked: '(Baldwin) has made no mistakes. He timed the election correctly in his Party's interest. Six months hence and it is certain the results would have been less favourable to him.'[3]

The innate sense of timing possessed by Attlee and Baldwin, and indeed by Harold Macmillan and Harold Wilson in other circumstances, was unfortunately not possessed by Edward Heath in 1974. At the time it appeared that Heath was almost determined to pursue a course of needless self-destruction. Let us go back a little in history to see what led to Heath's fatal decision in announcing a general election on 7 February 1974 for the 28th of that month.

Edward Heath had very real gifts which were recognized by Harold Macmillan when the latter made him his chief whip in December 1955 only five years after Heath became an MP, having won Bexley by 133 votes after a recount. In 1959 he was promoted to the Cabinet as Minister of Labour and in less than a year he became Lord Privy Seal with responsibility for Europe, a remarkable achievement for someone of such humble background, far removed from the 'magic circle' of Conservative leaders who at that time filled the higher echelons of power in the party.

Some sense of timing was at least apparent when Heath was asked why he had not stood for the leadership in October 1963 following Macmillan's retirement. He replied: 'It's not my time yet.' But when

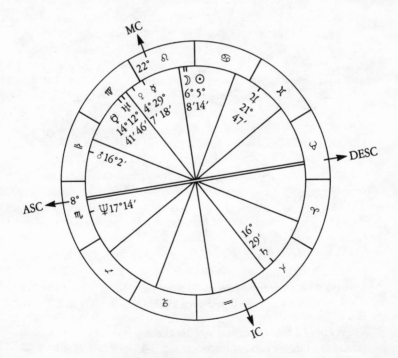

Figure 10.9 Horoscope for the election of Edward Heath as leader of the Conservative party
2.15 p.m. BST, 28 July 1965, London (51N32, 0)

Sir Alec Douglas-Home lost the election in October 1964 by five seats, the party decided they should look for someone more dynamic. Edward Heath was elected leader of his party at 2.15 p.m. on 28 July 1965 after a ballot on the previous day when he obtained a simple majority over Reginald Maudling and Enoch Powell.

The chart for Heath's election is given in Fig. 10.9. Here we find an elevated New Moon in Leo together with four planets in the 10th House. His natal Moon is also conjunct the Ascendant of this chart. There are no difficult aspects to the personal factors but there is a T-square involving Jupiter, Uranus, Pluto and Saturn, and Neptune is in the 1st House — rather too close to the Ascendant for comfort.

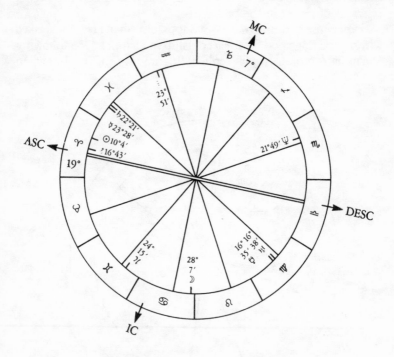

Figure 10.10 Horoscope for the general election
7 a.m. BST, 31 March 1966, London (51N32, 0)

When Harold Wilson called a general election on 31 March 1966 he gained the largest Labour victory since 1945 with a majority of 97 seats. It is of interest to compare this chart (see Fig. 10.10), for the start of the poll at 7 a.m. with that of Harold Wilson's own birth chart. Mars rises in Aries and we find a Grand Trine involving Neptune,

Saturn, Mercury and the Moon and also a T-square incorporating Jupiter, Uranus and Pluto, and again the Saturn–Mercury conjunction. This latter conjunction, which is involved in both patterns, lies close to Wilson's natal Sun.

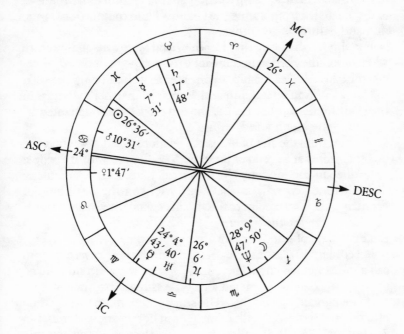

Figure 10.11 Horoscope for the general election
7 a.m. BST, 18 June 1970, London (51N32, 0)

On 18 May 1970, Wilson called another election which took place exactly one month later on 18 June, and the chart for this event is illustrated in Fig. 10.11. This time, in a comparatively unremarkable chart, Venus rises at 1 degree of Leo, exactly conjunct Heath's natal Neptune, and the Conservatives gained an overall majority of 30 seats. Edward Heath had become Prime Minister, the first Conservative to have achieved that office who had not been to a public school.

The times had become troubled by the beginning of 1972, particularly in the area of industrial relations. In this context we may note that Mars is in Virgo in the 6th House in Heath's natal chart which is square his Mercury in the 3rd – communicating was never one of Heath's strong points, especially where the workers were concerned, even though he had been Macmillan's Minister of Labour, and subsequently Secretary of State for Trade and Industry under Douglas-Home in October 1963. This Mars is also close to Jupiter in the chart of his leadership election but that in turn forms the apex of the T-square incorporating the Uranus–Pluto conjunction on one side and Saturn on the other.

It is also worth noting that Heath's natal Mars was square Saturn when he lost the election in February 1974, and it was opposite Jupiter when he lost the leadership a year later as well as being opposed to Harold Wilson's natal Sun and Margaret Thatcher's Uranus. In the chart for his lost leadership, the 6th House is also tenanted by Neptune, the Moon and Uranus.

Apart from the area of industrial relations, conflict was brewing on other fronts at the end of January 1972. On the 30th, 13 people were killed in Londonderry. We may recall that this is a particularly difficult time generally in the solar cycle, and the beginning of February is the lowest point of the year in general. As we watch events unfold, we can see the pattern of Heath's downfall taking place in the early days of one February after another.

In February 1972, the miners' strike provoked the government to call a state of emergency. Then in 1973 there was a second miners' strike. The Coal Board offered a pay rise so high that there was no room for bargaining and the NUM stuck out for more pay at a time of acute fuel shortages, with power cuts in homes and factories. On 7 February 1974, Heath called the general election. As an example of bad timing, he could hardly have made a worse choice. On the very same day, a special investigation into wage relativities by the Pay Board was promised, which had the inevitable effect of confusing the public who failed to see why an election should be necessary in those circumstances.

In addition to the industrial situation, the general state in the country was no better. There were high prices, huge rises in land values and an alarming trade gap. In the grip of a cold winter any government in power would have found it difficult to expect warm support from its followers. Moreover, the issue of a confrontation with the miners was no longer a viable basis for a contest in view of the negotiations proposed on the very day the election was called.

The poll on 28 February heralded the demise of Heath's power. The election itself was very close. The Conservatives held 296 seats with a majority of the votes, but Labour gained 301, the Liberals took 14 while the combined Scottish Nationalist, Welsh Nationalists and Ulster Unionists polled 20. There was therefore no overall majority but, having failed to come to an arrangement with the Liberals, Heath resigned on 4 March and Harold Wilson was again Prime Minister.

As Nigel Fisher wrote in *The Tory Leaders*: 'Timing is the essence of politics, as of so many other things in life.'[4] And of this election, he continued: 'There had, however, been much doubt about the timing of the election.' Robert Blake put it more forcefully: 'If Heath had called the election earlier, as some of his colleagues advised, he might have won on a programme of "Who governs Britain?" Having missed that option, he could have supported a case for special concessions to the miners in view of the oil crisis and a plausible if specious offer till as late as June 1975.'[5]

We can see in the chart of this election, in Fig. 10.12, that Saturn squares Heath's natal Mars, and Pluto is in exact opposition to his

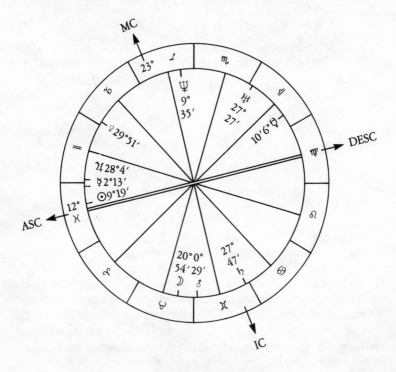

Figure 10.12 Horoscope for the general election
7 a.m. GMT, 28 February 1974, London (51N32, 0)

Ascendant as well as being in square aspect to his Venus–Pluto conjunction. In the chart of the election itself, Saturn lies close to the IC and is stationary. When Wilson called another election in October 1974, which he won by an overall majority of three seats, the Conservatives decided that enough was enough. Heath had lost three out of four elections in nine years and an election for the leadership of the party was demanded.

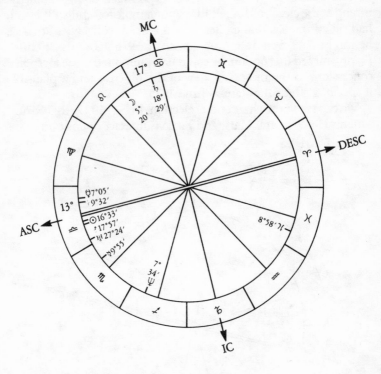

Figure 10.13 Horoscope for the general election
7 a.m. BST, 10 October 1974, London (51N32, 0)

In the chart for the general election on 10 October 1974, given in Fig. 10.13, we see Saturn at the Midheaven and a great emphasis on the Ascendant. The Sun–Mars conjunction rises in Libra with a close Venus–Pluto conjunction in the 12th House, the former making a close square aspect to Heath's natal Sun–Saturn conjunction. The leadership for the Conservative party again took place at the beginning of February, in 1975, the voting starting at noon on the 4th. Heath resigned after the first ballot, although

Margaret Thatcher failed to gain an overall majority, the figures being: Thatcher 130, Heath 119 and Hugh Fraser 16.

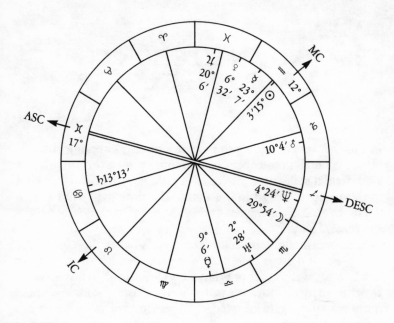

Figure 10.14 Horoscope for the Conservative party leadership contest Noon GMT, 4 February 1975, London (51N32, 0)

The chart for Heath's lost leadership is given in Fig. 10.14. On this occasion we see Saturn close to Heath's natal Sun, opposite Mars and forming a T-square with Pluto. The year 1974 itself had produced a catalogue of personal disasters for Heath, who was feeling the effects of his second Saturn Return. Not only had he lost the premiership of Britain and two general elections, but his yacht *Morning Cloud* had foundered in a storm and his godson, to whom he had been greatly attached, had been drowned. As if these tragedies were not enough, his home had been damaged by a bomb and he had nowhere to live.[6]

11.

CREATING AN ELECTION CHART – A WORKING EXAMPLE

In this chapter I am going to provide a practical working example of an electional horoscope. The enterprise will be the founding of a residential college for the study of astrology, the first of its kind in this country, indeed in the world. The time span will be from 8 a.m. to 8 p.m. on any day from 1 April to 30 September 1989, the place, London.

First, the preliminary considerations. What is the aim of the enterprise? If there is more than one aim, what are the subsidiary aims? What is the order of priority for these aims? In other words, what are we trying to achieve with this enterprise? The main purpose must be to propagate knowledge. Other aims will be to encourage individual thought and research, to bring together those interested in astrology in different parts of the world, and to enable astrology to be accepted more as a serious subject.

We know the time span so we are limited to choosing a date within that period. Are there any other charts, natal or mundane, which should be taken into account? I have deliberately taken an impersonal enterprise that is not tied to any individual as an example. For the purpose of this example, therefore, we shall not be comparing the electional chart with that of anyone or anything else. Nevertheless this is a question that must be raised at the outset.

It may be that the founder of the college intended to run it as his own private venture. It may be that the college was to be founded as the organ of a body that would control it. In either of these situations the charts of the individual or the organization would be of great importance. However, the college itself must be an independent entity for once the founder has died, once even the body has passed away, the college will continue to exist. It would therefore be quite wrong to tie the college to any individual although there should naturally be compatibility between the chart of the college and those involved in its welfare.

So much for the preliminary considerations. Now let us look at the factors that must be taken into account. The aim, or main aim, of the enterprise, will determine the planet which rules the enterprise. We have decided that the main aim is to be the propagation of knowledge. Therefore the planet ruling the enterprise will be Mercury. Where then should this planet be placed? To begin with we shall look at its position in the Zodiac and then see if aspects are made which need to be emphasized or avoided. According to general principles, the most appropriate place for Mercury is in Virgo, the Sign of its exaltation, and especially 15 degrees of that Sign.

The second best places in general terms would be the Signs of its rulership, Gemini and again Virgo, the yang and yin forces respectively. Now, so far as a college of astrology is concerned, what particular qualities do we want for the propagation of this type of learning? Virgo would be too down to earth to be ideal although it would be a possibility. Gemini, on the other hand, representing the principle of communication between people and the exchange of ideas, would be more appropriate. Aquarius, as another Air Sign and more directly related to progressive ideas, would be even better.

Now let us see what choice there is for Mercury in the six months under consideration. On 1 April Mercury is at 8 degrees of Aries and during the course of that period it passes through Taurus, Gemini, Cancer, Leo, Virgo, and gets as far as 10 degrees of Libra before moving back into Virgo. Having noted those positions we can see that it would be impossible to have Mercury in Aquarius, assuming we decided that was its best position. Of these seven Signs we shall choose Gemini as the most appropriate. As an Air Sign, it is concerned with communication, with people and ideas as opposed to the more factual knowledge of Virgo. Moreover, Gemini represents the yang, or giving, side of Mercury's rulership and in this enterprise the college will be concentrating on giving or providing knowledge and education to others rather than receiving it. The second best Sign would be Libra. This is another Air Sign, which is also concerned with communicating and with people. In addition, it is a Cardinal Sign which would help the flow of ideas.

Leo would be a possibility but it may encourage too much rigidity in clinging to autocratic ideas rather than encouraging individual thought. Aries would be too impulsive although again this Sign is a possibility as it would at least encourage new ideas. Taurus would be far too fixed and pedantic and Cancer too emotional for clarity of thought. Having looked at the Signs, we shall return to Mercury after we have looked at the other factors, and at that time we shall take account of its aspects, noting in particular the positions of Pluto, Neptune, Uranus and Saturn.

What about the subsidiary aims of this enterprise? Uranus would be relevant for encouraging individual thought and research, Venus for providing harmony among the staff and students, and the Sun for appealing to those in authority. There is effectively no choice with regard to Uranus. During the whole period of six months it only covers some five degrees as it turns retrograde during the latter half of April.

Venus and the Sun will always lie close to Mercury, so if Mercury is regarded as the ruler, and therefore of prime importance, these two bodies will be confined to follow in its wake. Venus covers rather more ground here than Mercury, starting at 10 degrees of Aries and ending up at 20 degrees of Scorpio. Both the Signs of its rulership, Taurus and Libra, are incorporated in this period. The latter would be more appropriate for the purposes of bringing people together, and it is also its yang Sign which would be apt in an enterprise which concentrates on giving. We shall look at the Sun's position separately when we consider the solar cycle.

We could also mention other, less important, aims ruled by other planets – the serious aspect of the subject, the expansiveness of the venture, the esoteric or spiritual side and others which would include Saturn, Jupiter and Neptune. However, we should beware of being tempted along too many minor paths. I have deliberately confined this exercise to the main aim and a strict order of subsidiary aims. If we allow ourselves to be diverted by others, we shall be in danger of trying to incorporate all the planets as co-rulers and end up with chaos.

The second consideration is to decide what quality we want for the enterprise. Here again we must be aware of our aim, or aims, and decide on the quality or qualities which will meet these. What then is the main quality we want for a residential college of astrology? The communication of progressive ideas should be paramount. Others should include a congenial community if the college is to endure and not be broken up by animosity or split by divisive factions. Enthusiasm, endurance, spiritual depth, human caring, tolerance are other qualities we should look for and encourage

In order to arrange these qualities we look chiefly at the position of the Moon and then at the personal planets. We can also look at the Ascendant although we shall examine this point separately in another context as we shall the Sun. In theory we could look at the

outer planets but in a period of six months it would not be possible
to activate even one Sign. Pluto moves through less than three degrees
of Scorpio, Neptune less than three degrees of Capricorn, Uranus,
as we have seen, no more than five degrees, and Saturn only about
six degrees of Capricorn. Even Jupiter moves only from the beginning
of Gemini to the beginning of Cancer.

For the communication of progressive ideas, Aquarius would be
most appropriate. Gemini and Libra would also be possibilities. For
a congenial atmosphere, Libra would be apt, Sagittarius would be
best for enthusiasm as would Leo and Aries, Capricorn or Taurus
would be good for endurance, and Pisces and Cancer for spiritual
depth and human caring.

We should therefore try to arrange for the Moon to be in Aquarius
if possible and bear in mind the other Signs for the personal planets,
and the Sun and Ascendant, if these do not conflict with other needs.
Naturally there may be a conflict of principle with the rulers of the
enterprise which we have discussed above and also of practice
depending on the time span available.

The third consideration relates to the cycles of the Sun, Moon and
the earth. Here we come to the seasons in the Sun's cycle, the phases
of the Moon in the lunar cycle and, to a much lesser extent, the times
of the day in the diurnal cycle. Let us start then with the solar cycle
which we examined at some length in Chapter 5. Here we can decide
what season is most suitable for this kind of enterprise and also what
part of the solar cycle should be avoided, bearing in mind the
notorious crisis points we have noted during the year.

Founding a college is a beginning, a new venture. Therefore the
yang half of the year should be chosen from the vernal to the
autumnal equinox. There is in any case little choice here although
it would be possible to choose a date around the autumn equinox
if that was thought to be appropriate. Spring is the time for
beginnings, summer for fruition. Spring would therefore be more
apt. Of the three Signs available, Aries or Gemini would be preferable
to Taurus. Taurus in any event is too slow and stable to be ideal for
this kind of venture although we do want an element of stability
and endurance for the college to survive. The middle of Taurus, as
one of the cross-quarter crisis periods, should certainly be avoided.

If we are to choose between Aries and Gemini, we need to decide
whether we want to emphasize the very early part of the cycle with
the onrush of energy or the more flexible part when the energies
have passed their middle phase of consolidation. From the practical
point of view we would also need to bear in mind the placing of

Mercury and, to a lesser extent, Venus, as these planets lie close to the Sun's path.

Although spring would be the most appropriate part of the solar cycle, summer would not be entirely inappropriate. Cancer marks another kind of beginning and with its qualities of protectiveness and caring would be suitable in general terms for a college. The summer, too, is a time of greater stability than the spring as the energies reach their zenith and begin to steady. Leo has the radiant quality of leadership and authority which would have its advantages although it would not be wholly compatible with a free exchange of ideas. Virgo, too, as the meticulous side of learning, would be a possibility, though the factual side of the establishment would be over-emphasized for a venture of this kind.

Taking all these matters into consideration, and especially the fact that we are creating something entirely new, the first of its kind in that no residential college of astrology exists, spring would certainly be the most appropriate part of the year for this particular venture.

The lunar cycle can now be looked at, and in this context I mean the phases of the Moon which, as I have pointed out, are simply the aspects between the Sun and the Moon. Far too much weight has been given to this factor in the past with unfortunate results in practice, for, if we make the Moon's phase our starting point, it is unlikely that we shall be able to choose the appropriate Sign for one of these bodies. For instance, if we are choosing a time during April and we have the Sun in Aries and then we decide we must have the Moon in a waxing trine to the Sun, we have no choice but to place it in Leo. In this position the Moon may also make difficult aspects which are fatal to the enterprise.

However, if it is possible to get the Moon in its best phase, it will be advisable to do so. The same principles apply here as in the case of the solar cycle. This is a yang enterprise, the beginning of a new venture, giving out knowledge to others, so it should take place during the waxing phase of the Moon. If possible it should be during the first quarter, avoiding the times around the hard aspects mentioned above.

The diurnal phase is also relevant to some extent but in practice its importance is very slight. Here too there will almost inevitably be conflict with more important factors – the Angles and the position of the Sun. The time of day is analogous to the cycles of the Sun and Moon and on that basis this enterprise is one that should take place during the day and if possible during the morning. That means that the Sun should be in the south-east quadrant.

Where the diurnal cycle is of real importance is with regard to the Angles and Houses. Here we are involved in the mundane sphere of the enterprise and can see what is likely to happen in the various areas of the venture. We can ensure that certain factors are placed in appropriate Houses and close to the Angles which strengthen particular areas. And we can try to avoid specific conflicts by ensuring that the planets themselves, and those making difficult aspects, are not placed in certain Houses.

The Ascendant, as we have seen, is also one of the measurements of time which activates the quality of the Sign it is in. We can therefore ensure that a particular quality is brought into play by having the Ascendant in a congenial Sign. In general terms, this will be a useful consideration, especially in balancing the Sign we have chosen for the Moon. For example, we may want a combination of communication and stability and arrange for the Moon to be in Gemini and the Ascendant in Taurus. However, it must be born in mind that in doing this we are limiting the position of the Moon in the diurnal cycle. In this example it can only be in the 1st or 2nd Houses because of the Sign on the Ascendant.

In particular the Sign on the Ascendant symbolizes the quality of the beginning of the enterprise and as such is an important factor. How important it is from this viewpoint depends on the significance of the start of a particular enterprise. As we have seen, the launching of a space probe will depend far more on its inception than would the building of a city. In these circumstances, the Ascendant will not be of major significance in founding a college, but from the general point of view of the beginning of the enterprise, which represents its immediate direction, it will be of great importance.

In accordance with general astrological principles, the beginning of any event, whether it be a human birth or the coming into being of a new state, will always describe its immediate attunement to the world. Thus the child that is born with Taurus rising, will not only be born slowly, but his whole relationship with the outside world will be steady and enduring. The Mode of the rising Sign will in particular determine the speed and quality of the enterprise. A Cardinal Sign would provide thrust, activity and rapidity, a Fixed Sign gives endurance and long-term stability but also rigidity and dogmatism, while a Mutable Sign gives flexibility but possible weakness.

So what qualities do we want for a residential college of astrology? We want the enterprise to last but we also want it to be foward-looking and active, encouraging new ideas, broadening its horizons, and helping to bring about a spirit of unity and understanding among its members and other people. While a Mutable Sign has associations with learning and flexibility, it is unlikely to last, and while a Fixed Sign has the required stability for a long-term enterprise, it may all too easily become stultified and rigid. A Cardinal Sign would therefore be best. Which one we choose depends on the Signs chosen for the other factors. Ideally Libra would provide the communication and harmony we are looking for but if we already have a sufficient emphasis on the Air Signs we may find another one more suitable.

We now come to the other Angles and the Houses. Here we can try to emphasize certain areas on the one hand, and avoid particular conflicts on the other. The Midheaven should be emphasized because it relates to the success of the enterprise in terms of public standing and recognition. This is of particular importance because we are trying to ensure that the teaching of astrology in general, and this college in particular, is accepted. Acceptance by those in authority would be helped by having the Sun close to the Midheaven; the Moon's position there would ensure public prestige, while Mercury's, both as the ruler of the enterprise and as the planet representing communications, would help to get the message across to a wider public.

The Descendant and the 7th House are important from the point of view of how the enterprise comes across to others on a one-to-one basis, and after the 10th House it is one of the most positive areas for factors that are concerned with communicating to others. So this would be an alternative area for the Sun or Moon. Conversely, because these are areas of particular importance, difficult planets should on all account be kept out of the 10th and 7th Houses and from any close proximity to the Midheaven and Descendant. Mars here, for example, would produce controversy, while Neptune would create confusion.

The 9th House is a significant area for this enterprise. In general it leads on to the 10th for it represents the dream or vision that manifests in the material success of the 10th. In particular it has associations with higher learning and communicating ideas to a wider audience which is clearly relevant here. If the Sun were to be placed in the 10th, then with Mercury and Venus close by one or even both of the latter could be placed in the 9th House.

All the Angles are powerful and therefore great care needs to be exercised with factors close to them. Even Jupiter close to the Ascendant in the 1st House has not been as helpful as some have supposed as we saw in the elected chart for Burma which was especially chosen for that position. We have also noted that the chart for the bombing of Hiroshima had this position and, while some may argue the necessity of this act, the beginning of the nuclear age can hardly merit unmitigated approval.

As opposed to the Midheaven and Descendant which should if possible contain planets beneficial to the enterprise, it is better to leave the 1st and 4th Houses empty. On no account should difficult planets, or even planets making difficult aspects, be placed near an Angle, especially near the Ascendant or IC. The 1st and 4th Houses are really extensions of the Angles and therefore the further away these planets are from the beginning of these Houses the less harm will be done.

The Houses representing communication should also be looked at with care. We have mentioned the 9th House in connection with higher education and the opposite House, the 3rd, will be relevant for the students. It is more a question here of trying to ensure that important Houses are not involved in problems with difficult planets or planets which make difficult aspects, although we should also bear in mind that it would be suitable to place important factors in these Houses if they cannot be placed in their ideal positions.

The 6th House is concerned with work and the personnel of the college; the 11th will be relevant for spreading ideas and for group work; and the 5th will emphasize creative work, and the germination of ideas into work that can be published. Some care should be taken with the 12th House which reflects hidden problems and the 2nd and 8th which relate to the financial position of the establishment.

Because of the limitations that are involved in the actual choice, it is often more a question either of trying to avoid the worst problems with the Angles and Houses, or at least of being aware of them. After all, if Neptune signifies confusion and delay, it will have to be placed somewhere. This is not to take a negative view of the factors but rather an objective one. Neptune, for example, like any factor, has its positive side and is important in inducing spirituality and artistic sensibility. But, as in any form of mundane astrology, the dangers do need to be born in mind.

Therefore we should try to keep obvious problems away from the central areas of the chart. These considerations apply as much to the aspects as to the planets themselves. It is unlikely that we can avoid all difficult aspects and therefore it is vital that we are aware of their order of importance. The Moon takes absolute precedence. On no account should the Moon be in hard aspect to Pluto, Neptune, Uranus, Saturn or Mars. Even Jupiter may provide problems.

Applying aspects are worse than those which are separating and the closer the orb the more difficult the situation will be. As the basic rule is that the planet which aspects another modifies the latter with the quality of the former, in theory a hard aspect from one of the above mentioned planets could be useful.

A square from Neptune to the Moon would provide a quality of sensitivity which could induce spirituality and heightened imagination as well as the more negative qualities of confusion and deceit. It may be possible to use these qualities positively therefore, but great care should always be taken. The soft aspects, the trines and sextiles, will provide some strength but their importance is slight. Moreover, it will seldom be that a soft aspect can be incorporated without sacrificing a more important principle in the process. But if trines and sextiles can be made to relevant planets, well and good. In practice the best way to strengthen the Moon and other factors is by placing them in strong areas of the diurnal cycle, close to the Midheaven, for example.

After the Moon, the ruling planet (which in this case will be Mercury) is the most important factor, and then, the Sun, Venus and Mars. Once again, hard, especially applying, aspects from the outer planets should if possible be avoided. There will frequently be times when the outer planets are in mutual aspect and in those cases there is greater danger because more than one planet will aspect another at the same time. During the period under consideration, Saturn, Uranus and Neptune are in conjunction at the beginning of Capricorn, so any planet at the beginning of a Cardinal Sign will make a hard aspect to this multiple conjunction.

These, then, are the separate factors which should be taken into account. In synthesizing them into an appropriate chart we need to balance the various qualities and principles that are desirable in our enterprise. We may feel, for example, that the quality of communication is ideal and therefore emphasize Gemini. But although this may be the best quality, we shall not want every factor to be in this one Sign. So we must bear in mind other qualities in an order of importance. Communication, if we like, is the primary concern, but stability for long-term endurance, human empathy and enthusiasm are also qualities that will, as a whole, produce the best chart for the enterprise.

It is unlikely that any chart will be ideal in the sense that there will be no problem areas and every factor will be placed in the best Sign, the most appropriate House and will make the most beneficial aspects. We can only choose a pattern as it actually exists in the sky at any particular moment. But, if we use the precepts I have just listed, we can certainly arrange the best time within these limits, and we can also be aware of the difficulties that may arise.

So let us sum up the points made above and choose the time for founding the first residential college of astrology. We start with the ruler of the enterprise, Mercury. We have decided that, of the Signs available between April and September, Gemini would be the most appropriate. This in itself limits the time to between 30 April and 28 May or from 12 June to 5 July. The subsidiary ruler, Venus, would, we decided, be best in Libra but that would not be possible given the period that Mercury is in Gemini.

The four Signs available for Venus are Taurus, Gemini, Cancer and Leo. Taurus would provide some stable balance and is also one of the Signs ruled by Venus, although it represents its yin energy. Cancer would provide human empathy, and Leo enthusiasm and radiance. Gemini would also be a possibility although it would be better not to emphasize one Sign too much. However, we should just bear in mind the possibilities for Venus while we look at the other factors.

The quality of the enterprise from the descriptive viewpoint depends mainly on the Sign of the Moon. We have mentioned Aquarius as the best Sign for this purpose which would mean either 25 to 27 May or from 21 to 23 June. The Sun would be in either Gemini or Cancer at these times while Venus would be in either of these Signs as well. Mars would be in either Cancer or Leo. From the point of view of balance, the latter dates would therefore be more suitable, otherwise we would have the Sun, Mercury and Venus all in Gemini. Furthermore, Mars is not well placed in Cancer which is the Sign of its fall, whereas it would provide a sense of creative drive in Leo.

Looking now at the cycles of the Sun and Moon, we find that the Sun's position has already been chosen by the previous principles. If these principles conflict to any major extent with the most appropriate part of the solar cycle we should reassess the situation. We have decided that the best time would be the yang half of the year from spring to the autumn equinox and ideally the spring would be best and Gemini the ideal time during the spring. However, too great an emphasis on Gemini, or any one Sign, would not be wise, and Cancer as a Cardinal Sign concerned with caring and protectiveness would provide an excellent balance. So again the period between 21 and 23 June would be suitable. Midsummer itself is one of the crisis times although not a period of major problems, but if possible we should choose a date after Midsummer Day which falls on the 21st in 1989.

From the Sun's cycle, we move on to that of the Moon. The Moon's phase is not ideal as it is in its waning period but this is a relatively minor point. What is of greater significance is that there is the lack of any hard aspect between the lights. We may even be able to go one step further here and arrange for a trine aspect between the Sun and Moon.

We can now turn to the diurnal cycle. Here we need to balance the best area for the Sun, Moon and Mercury and also the other planets on the one hand with the most appropriate Sign for the Ascendant on the other. If we choose Libra as the rising Sign, which would be ideal, we would have the Sun, and indeed Mercury and Venus, close to the Midheaven, which would again be ideal. Can we also ensure that the Moon is as strong as possible and that there are no major problems with the other Angles or important Houses?

We have now arrived at a date from between 21 to 23 June. On the 21st the Moon is square Mars and on the 22nd it is square Pluto. So what about the 23rd? No difficult aspects are made on that day and the Moon is also trine Jupiter and coming up to a trine with the Sun on the 24th. It therefore looks as if we have narrowed the time down to 23 June.

If we want Libra rising, we can have a time between about 12.54 p.m. and 3.43 p.m. BST. The beginning of this period would be good from the point of view of having the Sun close to the Midheaven but it would also mean that Uranus, and to a lesser extent Neptune and Saturn, would be close to the IC which would create difficulties. Fortunately, although Saturn, Uranus and Neptune are close together, the Sun is only opposite Uranus which is not entirely inappropriate for a new venture in astrology.

Where would the Moon be at these times? At 1 p.m. BST it would be in the 5th House as indeed it would be at 2 p.m. Here we have to make a choice. If the Moon is to be in Aquarius and we want the Sun on the Midheaven, then the Moon will have to be in the 5th House. Indeed if we want a Libran Ascendant and the Moon in Aquarius, we will have confined the Moon to the 5th or perhaps the end of the 4th House. In addition, by having the Ascendant in Libra, we also have the Sun, together with Mercury and Venus, near the Midheaven.

The decision then becomes a choice between keeping Libra as the rising Sign and ensuring that neither the Midheaven nor the IC is afflicted by difficult planets. The danger to the IC comes from the concentration of Saturn, Uranus and Neptune from 4 to 12 degrees of Capricorn, while that to the Midheaven comes, albeit to a much lesser extent, from Mars at 5 degrees of Leo. Nor do we want the Moon close to the IC. If we have the beginning of Libra rising we will have the Saturn–Uranus–Neptune conjunction on the IC, while if we have the end of that Sign on the Ascendant, Mars will be conjunct the Midheaven.

In the circumstances we need an Ascendant between these two points. We shall therefore take 21 degrees of Libra for the Ascendant which gives 28 degrees of Cancer as the Midheaven. While Mars makes a somewhat wide conjunction to the Midheaven, this also puts Venus close to the Midheaven and ensures that the difficult conjunction in Capricorn is not only outside the 4th House but also not conjunct the IC, which is the most important consideration. The 3rd House, which relates to the students, is not the best place for this conjunction, but as a Cadent House it is comparatively weak and it may also be

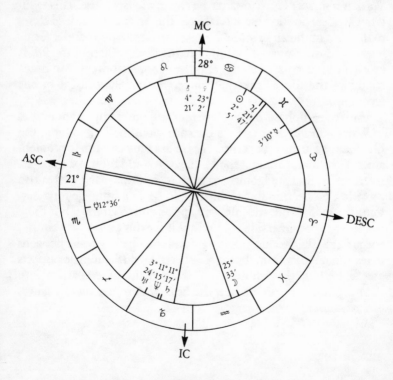

Figure 11.1 Example of an electional horoscope
2.54 p.m. BST, 23 June 1989, London (51N32, 0)

possible to harness its positive qualities.

This time also means that the Moon will be in the 5th House of creativity which, while not the best place in an absolute sense, is certainly a good position. What is of greater importance is that the Moon is in the ideal Sign. It makes no difficult aspects and makes a fairly close trine to Jupiter. The Moon also forms a wide Grand Trine incorporating both the Sun and the Ascendant. From these points of view the Moon's position could hardly be improved.

In addition the Sun is well placed in the 9th House of further education. A balance is achieved between communication and ideas with the emphasis on the Air Signs, caring and human concern with the Sun, Venus and the Midheaven in Cancer, and creativity and enthusiasm with Mars in Leo in the 10th. Certainly this establishment will be able to carve its own way with forcefulness and individuality with its strong Mars and the Sun opposing Uranus.

The completed chart for 2.54 p.m. BST is illustrated in Fig. 11.1. We may also note Pluto towards the end of the 1st House. This again is not an ideal position but it is far from the Ascendant, indeed closer to the cusp of the 2nd House. It makes no hard aspects and it forms a sextile to the Saturn–Neptune conjunction. Jupiter in the 9th is excellent for higher learning, and the concentration of important factors at the top of the chart augers extremely well for public recognition.

With the emphasis on the Air Signs and other important bodies in Water and Fire Signs, there is a corresponding lack so far as the Element of Earth is concerned. There are only two other problem areas. First, Mars conjunct the Midheaven could induce some over-assertiveness and antagonism as a result, but this placing does also provide a pioneering spirit which could be an advantage for a new foundation. Second, the Sun is in opposition to Uranus, but there is also a very positive side to this aspect for this particular venture, encouraging the breaking of new ground and opening wider horizons in learning. Apart from those two aspects, no difficult major aspects are formed in the whole chart. Taking all these matters into consideration, we can see how the best chart in the circumstances can be chosen.

12.
THE WEB OF LIFE

Whatever befalls the earth befalls the sons of the earth. Man did not weave the web of life, he is merely a strand in it. Whatever he does to the web, he does to himself.

Chief Seattle

In *For the Record: From Wall Street to Washington*, Donald Regan, sacked Chief of Staff to the USA President, wrote: 'Virtually every major move and decision the Reagans made during my time as White House Chief of Staff was cleared in advance with a woman in San Francisco who drew up horoscopes.'[1] The kind of astrology used by President Reagan was specifically electional: choosing the right time for the summit meeting with Mikhail Gorbachev at Reykjavik, arranging his itinerary with other world leaders, deciding on the days which were right, as well as those to avoid, for important business.

Has the wheel come full circle? Have the leaders of the world now reached the stage where they realize the importance of timing in their lives? It would be tempting to believe that Chief Seattle's vision has been vindicated by the successors of the race who destroyed his heritage. Unfortunately, this is far from being the case.

There is now a growing awareness of the importance of time. The advent of chronotherapy, the discovery by scientists of the changing quality and effects of time in animate as well as inanimate organisms, has led to the acceptance of time as a real dimension of life. This acceptance, on an intuitive level, has always existed among 'primitive' people. We must hope that its acceptance today will enable modern man to come to a proper understanding of his place in the world.

We saw in Chapter 2 that there are two prerequisites for the development of electional astrology: belief in the freedom to choose, together with an understanding of man's relationship with time. Originally, man was in touch with nature as well as with time as an aspect of nature, but his belief in the freedom to choose was lacking.

So man was at the mercy of nature and the aspects of nature that he personalized in his gods. When the gods died man was at the mercy of himself. Now we have learned the secrets of the earth and have discovered freedom. But, in doing so, we have lost our union with nature. Instead of being controlled by nature, we control it, exploit it, manipulate it for our own ends.

The Red Indians in their primitive wisdom knew man's place in the world. They knew the balance that had to be maintained for their survival in that world and for the survival of the world in their hands. Chief Seattle knew, at the time he wrote the words I have quoted above, that his time and the time of his people was over. He knew that the white man was 'a stranger who comes in the night and takes from the land whatever he needs', and that 'the earth is not his brother, but his enemy, and when he has conquered it, he moves on'.

Having the freedom to choose, without knowing the pattern of the universe in which those choices are necessarily made, produces a sense of alienation. Men come and go, like the waves of the sea. Man, and the world of which he is a part, changes and develops in time. If man is a part of the world, instead of being apart from it, he will make his choices freely within the pattern of time that exists beneath the surface of events. Otherwise he can only fight against his own nature and the greater nature of which he is, knowingly or unknowingly, a part.

There are those who will ask: What is the practical use of electional astrology? There are those, too, who will ask: What is the meaning of electional astrology? Where does it lead? Electional astrology is, first and foremost, a practical science. It begins with specific issues that occur in our daily lives. Then, from a deeper understanding of the physical world, we may be led to a profounder wisdom of existence.

Electional astrology is useful, in so far as it enables us to choose the right time for our actions and for the enterprises that are born in time. In his article in *The Times* on 18 May 1988, Woodrow Wyatt made the point that President Reagan was remarkably successful nationally and internationally. 'Perhaps we should be grateful,' he wrote, 'that seemingly he relies more on advice from astrologers than from political commentators.'

Electional astrology is meaningful, in so far as it enables us to discover our relationship with time as one of the strands of life. How then can we regain our relationship with time without losing our freedom of choice? To achieve this end, two things are necessary. The first depends on our understanding of the way in which time works, the second, on our attitude towards time. The difficulty scientists experienced in understanding time, and in even accepting its reality as a coordinate of nature like length and breadth, sprang from the fact that they could not see it, which in turn sprang from their materialistic assumption that nothing was real unless it could be weighed and measured.

Moreover, even when they came to recognize the varying qualities of time, their ability to correlate these variations, and hence to foresee them, was limited. Astrology, on the other hand, is the only system which provides an objective way of correlating the differing qualities of time in the form of the heavenly bodies which reflect both the cyclic and the descriptive nature of time. Astrology thus provides the means of understanding the way in which time works.

But simply understanding the mechanics of time through astrological symbolism will not provide us with the relationship that is necessary. Nor will mere understanding lead us to real freedom of choice. Newton regarded time as a river flowing by, a continuum that ran its unchanging course behind a changing world, and just another aspect of the universe which man could master.

That view of time, and of the universe as a whole, is no longer valid. If we are to find meaning in time, and in the world, then our attitude to time must change. Our approach to life is based on the events which occur in time. But in only seeing the events themselves we fail to recognize the pattern of which these evens are a part. The events, which appear as the only reality on the physical level, are, on a deeper level, merely the space element of the underlying pattern intruding in time.

If we are to discover meaning in time and in life, then we need to see the pattern itself. This is the web of life, and time is one of its strands. Then we can see what appear to be separate, meaningless occurrences in the perspective of our lives as a whole. We can see how they fit into the thread of our existence and where they are leading.

Electional astrology, then, rightly understood, enables us to see the pattern of the archetypal principles that govern life on all levels because this pattern is reflected in the motions of the heavenly bodies. Having seen that underlying pattern, we can learn to live according to its thread. And the more we, as individuals, learn to live in accordance with our own pattern, the more we become at one with the greater, universal pattern. In this way we will instinctively act at the right time and achieve the art of perfect timing.

We can, if we wish, retain the image of time as a river. But we cannot continue to regard ourselves as living on its bank, watching the river flow by. We are part of its stream, or, to return to that favourite image of the East, we row along its waters. All life, including our personal lives, develops in time. Events occur when the time is right. There is a right time, and a wrong time, for everything. Just as each human being is born under his or her own star, so each thing under the heavens is born under its own star, like the temple founded in Sumeria by King Gudea. Each business venture, each political party, each marriage, is born in heaven when its time is right.

By choosing the wrong time, we waste time fighting against the natural tides of the universe. And as each human being needs to develop according to his or her own life-span, so each enterprise needs to develop according to its inherent life-span. All things develop in time. The seed will not germinate in the winter, nor the plant wither in the spring. In human terms, the aim of life, and of therapy as a means of bringing people in touch with their lives, is to become ourselves, the selves that astrologically are reflected in our birth charts. The personal pattern which develops in time can be seen in the directions, the transits, the progressions that flow from that birth chart.

The need to accept this personal pattern was made clear by Jung when he wrote: 'Not wanting to live is synonymous with not wanting to die. Becoming and passing away are the same curve. Whoever does not accompany this curve remains suspended in the air and grows numb. From middle age on, only he remains alive who is willing to die with life.'

The universe too has its patterns in time. One of the most important lessons for man today is to recognize the reality of those patterns, which connect all forms of life on earth. When man originally, and intuitively, recognized the unity of the world around him, he reverenced his heritage. He regarded the land, the rivers, the sky as parts of his own life, as his brothers and sisters. For him all aspects of the earth were sacred. Although he acted as much from fear as from love, nevertheless his appreciation of the totality of the universe was real.

In separating man from his world, the love as much as the fear disappeared. With man set apart from nature, the world is now in grave danger as rich nations exploit their poor neighbours, as finite resources are destroyed, as the ozone level which protects our atmosphere is eroded, as land and sea are polluted. Only now is it beginning to dawn on man that nature is finely balanced, that the tides cannot always flow out, that whatever is done to one organism will affect another, that the trees which are being felled will produce soil erosion, drought and famine.

The universe in which our ancestors lived and that in which we live now is the same. It is our attitude towards it, and our knowledge of it, that determines our relationship with it. There was no free will when our ancestors' relationship was one of fear. In spite of a genuine love for the earth, there was no sense of equality between man and the forces of nature. But neither is there any genuine free will when man works against nature and treats the earth as his enemy. For nature, in all its aspects, the earth and humankind included, has its own momentum, its own life in time as well as in space. If we simply try to impose our wills and push in one direction against the tide, then in some way, at some later time, the tide will flow back again.

The purpose of electional astrology then is to provide a deeper understanding of the pattern of time in the universe, so that we can synchronize our personal lives with the greater life-pattern of the universe. I hope therefore that in the process of learning the practical craft of elections we will learn the greater art of being in touch with the time element of life. In so doing, we will change our perspective of life, and we shall be able to regain the sense of unity with the universe and with all forms of life that was an integral aspect of our ancestors' existence. In the process, nature will no longer be something 'out there', part of an alien world, but something inextricably a part of us.

'Is there not an appointed time to man upon the earth?' asked Job. The pattern of time exists beneath all things. Each human being, each living creature, each enterprise and undertaking born of human hands, has its appointed time. Each has its tides and it rises and falls and rises again. Man's life is a strand in that pattern. Astrology is the visual and symbolic means of seeing that pattern in its entirety. We can work with the personal tides that are our lives and with the greater tides that are the life of the universe. As the two blend into one, we can achieve, if we wish, the perfect timing that is ingrained in the whole. The choice is ours.

NOTES

Chapter 1
1. W. Shakespeare, *Julius Caesar*, 4.3.
2. W. Shakespeare, *Hamlet*, 4.5.
3. F. Weldon, *Praxis*, London, Hodder and Stoughton, 1978, p.17.
4. J. Campbell, *The Masks of God*, London, Souvenir Press (Educational & Academic) Ltd., 1974, p.118.
5. J.H. Newman, *Essay on the Development of Christian Doctrine*, London, 1878, p.48.
6. Quoted in W. Allen, *Tradition and Dream*, London, The Hogarth Press, 1986, p.3.
7. M. Grant, *Caesar*, London, Weidenfeld & Nicolson, 1974.

Chapter 2
1. Quoted in C.A. Burland, *The Gods of Mexico*, London, Eyre & Spottiswoode, 1967, p.150.
2. J. Lindsay, *Origins of Astrology*, London, Frederick Muller, 1971.
3. Quoted in J. Lindsay, ibid., p.2.
4. Quoted in A.L. Oppenheim, *Letters from Mesopotamia*, p.157.
5. Ibid., p.158.
6. D. Laertios, L. vii, p.87.
7. Tacitus, *Annals*, vi, p.20.
8. Quoted in M. and C.H.B. Quennell, *Everyday Life in Roman and Anglo-Saxon Times*, London, B.T. Batsford, 1959, p.151.
9. Quoted in R Gleadow, *The Origin of the Zodiac*, London, Jonathan Cape, 1968, p.56.
10. I. Khaldun, *The Mugaddimah: An Introduction to History*, translated by F. Rosenthal, London, Routledge & Kegan Paul, 1958, vol. II, p.211.
11. Quoted in L. MacNeice, *Astrology*, London, Aldus Books, 1964, p.153.

12. Ficino, *De Vita*, III, p.11.
13. Quoted in E. Garin, *Astrology in the Renaissance*, London, Routledge & Kegan Paul, 1983, p.40.
14. P.J. French, *John Dee*, London, Routledge & Kegan Paul, 1972, p.92.
15. E. Ashmole, *Theatrum Chemicum Brittanicum*, p.443.
16. K. Thomas, *Religion and the Decline of Magic*, Harmondsworth, Penguin Books Ltd., 1971, p.759.
17. Quoted in K. Thomas, op. cit., p.736.
18. Ibid., p.403.

Chapter 3
1. M. Gauquelin, *Astrology and Science*, London, Mayflower Books Ltd., 1972, p.221.
2. Quoted in M. Gauquelin, ibid., p.221.
3. St Bernardino of Siena, *Le prediche volgari dette nella piazza del Campo l'anno 1427*, ed. L. Bianchi, St Bernardino, Siena, 1880, vol. I, p.38.
4. M. Gauquelin, op. cit., p.221.
5. I Corinthians 15.41.

Chapter 4
1. L. Tzu, *Tao Te Ching*, The Richard Wilhelm edition, London, Routledge & Kegan Paul, 1985, p.30.
2. Ibid., p.17.
3. These principles are discussed at length in my two books, *The Marriage of Heaven and Earth*, London, Routledge & Kegan Paul, 1985, and *Astrotherapy*, London, Routledge & Kegan Paul, 1987.
4. Quoted in C.K. Anthony, *The Philosophy of the I Ching*, Stow, Anthony Publishing Co., 1981, p.3.
5. Ibid., p.95.

Chapter 5
1. J. Wechsberg, *Verdi*, London, Weidenfeld & Nicolson, 1974, p.21.
2. S. Morley, *Oscar Wilde*, London, Weidenfeld & Nicolson, 1976, p.105.
3. Quoted in R. Castleden, *The Wilmington Giant*, Wellingborough, Turnstone Press Ltd, 1983, p.144.
4. Ibid., p.185.

Chapter 8
1. V.E. Robson, *Electional Astrology*, New York, Samuel Weiser, 1972, p.32.

Chapter 9

1. V.E. Robson, *Electional Astrology*, New York, Samuel Weiser, 1972, p.14.

Chapter 10

1. W. Wyatt, 'The stars and me', *The Times*, 18 May 1988.
2. T. Burridge, *Clement Attlee*, London, Jonathon Cape, 1985, p.313.
3. H. Montgomery Hyde, *Neville Chamberlain*, London, Weidenfeld & Nicolson, 1976, p.81.
4. N. Fisher, *The Tory Leaders*, London, Weidenfeld & Nicolson, 1977, p.77.
5. R. Blake, *The Conservative Party from Peel to Thatcher*, London, Methuen, 1985, p.316.
6. The birth data of Edward Heath is: 11.55 p.m., 9 July 1916, Broadstairs, Kent. That of Harold Wilson is: 11 a.m., 11 March 1916, Huddersfield, Yorks. That of Margaret Thatcher is: 9 a.m., 13 October 1925, Grantham, Lincs.

Chapter 12

1. W. Wyatt, 'The stars and me', *The Times*, 18 May 1988.

INDEX

Of further interest . . .

ECLIPSES

The power points of astrology

Derek Appleby and Maurice McCann

Eclipses have been a source of wonder for man since the dawn of evolution, inspiring all manner of legends. But their importance astrologically has been long understated, despite their obvious effects on both the animal and vegetable kingdoms, and this book hopes to redress this balance.

Beginning with an explanation of the astronomical background to eclipses, the authors demonstrate how eclipses, lunations and pleniluna manifest in human experience. They show how the effects and potency of these phenomena can be calculated, and how they affect horoscopes when combined with other astrological influences.

Drawing upon dramatic historical events to demonstrate the validity of eclipses in the lives of both great people and humble citizens, ECLIPSES breaks new ground in Mundane Astrology. Also, by examining such pertinent questions as whether an eclipse has to be visible to be effective and how long the power of the eclipse degree persists in the cosmos, the book will inspire new lines of investigation for every serious astrologer.

Derek Appleby has been a practising astrologer for 20 years and is a leading teacher and lecturer in the field. He is former President of the Astrological Lodge of London and author of the seminal HORARY ASTROLOGY.

Maurice McCann has a BA (Hons) in the History of Astrology and is Chairman of the Astrological Lodge of London. He is co-director with Derek Appleby of The Meonen School, *a correspondence course in Horary Astrology.*